MW00620784

KINGDOM BUSINESS BOOKS VOL: 1

Author of the Bestseller: The Order of Melchizedek

THE

JOSEPH

OF

ARIMATHEA

CALLING

…Rediscovering Tools for Wealth Creation &
God's Highest Purpose for the Wealthy in His Kingdom!

By

Dr. Francis Myles

Kingdom Business Books – Vol 1

Published by
Francis Myles International
P.O. Box 2467, Scottsdale, AZ 85252

For Worldwide Distribution
Printed in the United States

Cover Design by Workin Perkin

Typesetting and Internal Design by Son Enterprises

Edited by Karen Hosey

Publisher is not responsible for websites (or their content)
if not owned by the publisher

Kingdom Business Books – Vol 1

Acknowledgments

WHAT WE BECOME IN GOD is a sum total of the divine encounters we have had, the people we have met, our experiences, and the books we have read. The saying "No man is an island" is certainly true in the context of authoring this book. I want to acknowledge the impact that the following men and women of God have had on my life:

- Carmela Real Myles for being the love of my life and an amazing glue and connector for God's Kingdom
- Dr. Ralph & Eileen Wilkerson and HRM King Adamatey I (my spiritual parents)
- Apostle Harrison Chileshe my pastor in Africa who taught me how to pray
- Apostle John Eckhardt who introduced me to the apostolic
- Dr. John P. Kelly who commissioned me as an apostle
- Dr. Jonathan David whose teachings have radically changed my life
- Pastor Tom Deuschle whose friendship and wise counsel continue to amaze me

- Dr. G.E. Bradshaw my covenant brother and spiritual covering
- Linda Vega and Karen Hosey who are living examples of this book's message
- Jeffrey Mzwimbi for being a true Joseph
- Bishop Robert Smith who introduced me to the message on the One New Man
- Dr. Bob Harrison America's Increase Authority
- Dr. Bruce Cook for introducing me to the world of marketplace leaders
- My parents, Daniel and Ester Mbepa, for raising me in the fear of the Lord (I will see you in heaven someday)
- Dr. Jesse Bielby for your prophecies that have guided me
- Prophet Gershom Sikaala your prophecies and friendship have refreshed me
- Members of Royal Priesthood International Embassy Tempe, Arizona

The teachings and personal conversations these men and women have had with me over the years have added to the richness of this book.

While the material in this book is original, there are a few quotes throughout that have been taken from the published works of other notable Christian authors. Each is documented in the Endnote section.

Endorsements

"If you are called as a modern-day Joseph or Daniel, an Esther or Lydia, then you will want to buy and study this dynamic, revelatory teaching dealing with the mindset and mantle of stewarding resources and influence. Dr. Francis Myles has done it again by delivering another masterpiece of literature. His latest book, The Joseph of Arimathea Calling, is packed with nuggets of wisdom and gems of truth that will help you unlock your future and access your destiny. Read this powerful book and you will gain valuable insights to help you grow and succeed in the marketplace. Then share it with your family and friends."

~ Dr. Bruce Cook, Founder
Kingdom House Publishing
Chief Executive Officer: Kingdom Congressional International Alliance
(KCIA)

"The insightful revelations in this informative book will give you a greater understanding of purpose and can launch a fresh wave of wealth creation in your life."

~ Dr. Bob Harrison
"America's Increase Authority"

"Dr. Francis Myles is one of the great modern masters of receiving revelation from the Holy Spirit on the Word of God, and translating that into meaningful texts, which have the power to activate his audience into ushering the Kingdom of God into the marketplace. His bestselling book <u>The Order of Melchizedek</u> is one such work, and the new <u>The Joseph of Arimathea Calling</u> is set to follow in its footsteps. Throughout <u>The Joseph of Arimathea Calling</u> Dr. Myles delivers to his readers an incredible depth of insight and understanding of the historical biblical events and their contemporary application in the marketplace. The high achievers and significant entrepreneurs of our society have been largely neglected and even avoided by the vocational church for decades, usually based on a misunderstanding of scripture that wealth is evil. Within his latest book Dr. Myles eradicates this stigma and sets free this extremely strategic demographic to invade the "top end of town" by using their wealth and influence to bring in the Gospel of the Kingdom. A must read for all marketplace participants."

~ Dave Hodgson, CEO
Paladin Corporation (Australia)
Founder and Leader of Kingdom Investors

"Dr. Francis Myles' <u>The Joseph of Arimathea Calling</u> revelation is by far the most impactful expression of supernatural economic energy since the release of his book <u>The Order of Melchizedek</u>. The wheels of the financial industry will rotate at high speed when this incredible information is released. The Body of Christ has not been short on vision but it has lacked the resources to see many visions realized. This book will end the drought by shining light on an all but obscure figure in biblical history. Dr. Myles' ability to bridge the historical gap between Joseph the patriarch and Joseph of Arimathea is astonishingly precise. This type of parallel can only be revealed through the supernatural intelligence of God's Spirit!"

~ Dr. Gordon E. Bradshaw
President – Global Effect Movers & Shakers Network and Kingdom
Author – I SEE THRONES! – Igniting and Increasing Your
Influence in the Seven Mountains of Culture

"Dr. Francis Myles is a unique voice in the marketplace with a unique mantle to demystify and give clarity to the relevance of those in the marketplace in God's universal plan. In this book, you will be equipped with practical wisdom to build influence and a legitimate cause to create wealth. In your hands is a mantle that will change your life forever!"

~ Dr Hosiah Tagara, Founder and President
WealthMasters Global
Johannesburg, South Africa

"This is a destiny altering book for those called to the highest levels of wealth in the Kingdom of God, and those also who truly seek to achieve such wealth and who seek to understand the different facets of such a high calling. I recommend this book to every Kingdom entrepreneur and those called to the highest levels of wealth and financial dominion. This book carries astounding and destiny altering revelations. This is a message for our generation where great wealth is increasingly strategic for the accomplishment of God's work on earth."

~ Dr. Walter Mandaza, Chairman
The Webcom Group of Companies
Sandton, South Africa

"Dr. Francis Myles courageously raises questions most preachers and writers conveniently ignore. I have not read a book on Joseph of Arimathea before and this book reveals the side of God and perspectives on biblical wealth that every Christian businessman should be exposed to. The lessons shared in the book are ones learnt in the deep places, in times of profound spiritual searching. The book dares ask tough questions of our age and then dares to deliver even tougher answers. Dr. Myles has a way of bringing to light our little religious games. Often times we don't mention our doubts so we tiptoe around the subject of bribes. This book is powerful because it tells the truth about bribes in a way that leaves you in no doubt."

~ Jeff Mzwimbi,
Meshullam Capital Partners
Zimbabwe

"This is a must read book especially for those who have been given a clear mandate from heaven to fund the Kingdom in the last days. I have heard many in the Body of Christ who have made statements, "I am called to be a Joseph." This book will exemplify that statement and give the Body of Christ a different perspective of what a "true Joseph" is through the life of Joseph of Arimathea. The Bible doesn't have very much to say about this New Testament Joseph in the life of Jesus. However, what was said about him is more than enough to impact and influence the lives of those whose quest for the truth and their purpose on earth is greater than their temptation to profit from the world. This revelation of Joseph's relationship with the Lord will prepare those whose prophetic word has not come to pass yet and give a deeper purpose to those who are already walking in this mandate."

~ Carmela Real Myles, Co-Pastor
Royal Priesthood International Embassy
Tempe, Arizona

"It never ceases to amaze me the depth of revelation Dr. Myles can get from an "obscure" passage of scripture that ultimately has life changing impact. I never would have thought there were 14 unique characteristics to that one man in that one passage of scripture that relates to current day Kingdom businessmen and women. Dr. Myles lays a sure foundation on why God needs us to not only be wealthy but to have influence so that we can be vessels used to advance the

Kingdom under the Order of Melchizedek. After reading about Joseph of Arimathea I am confident that a shift can take place *in my business as I embrace the Joseph of Arimathea calling."*

~ Karen Hosey, President
First Capital Solutions
Stockbridge, GA

"The opportunities and challenges of our time calls for a fresh look at wealth by all believers. Wealth can open doors that otherwise will be closed. God is not against wealth; that is very clear in scripture. What God is against is allowing wealth to control you. Dr. Myles clearly states this basic truth and purpose of wealth in this book. Every Christian needs to read this book and learn the truths it portrays and invite others to read it too."

~ David Asante, Senior Pastor
Bridge of Hope
Nashville, TN

"The timing on this book couldn't be better! Now, more than ever before, there is a need to understand the Lord's true plan for wealth, especially for those assigned to take the Mountain of Business and operate as a priest and king in the marketplace. The Joseph of Arimathea Calling offers new insight to building wealth and is a must read for all Christian entrepreneurs Dr. Francis Myles offers fresh revelation on how the Lord expects us to use wealth to make a difference in the Kingdom and has captured meaningful examples of this ancient wisdom in the life of Joseph. If you've ever questioned how to do business according to God's plan and find success in the marketplace, then this book is your answer!"

~ Flavia Schoffner, RN CCM CLNC CNML
Founder, Baruch International, PLLC
Phoenix, Arizona

Foreword

The world as we know it today has changed many times and at a velocity that man can hardly fathom, let alone control. This also points to the fact that change is continuous and unending – whether positive or negative. Change is never neutral or partial, and neither fears nor takes direction from anyone. It doesn't ask for permission or approval, but best functions with those who cooperate with it and align accordingly.

As is change, so is purpose. God is a God of purpose and everything He has created, He set it to operate within purpose. Therefore, humankind is born with a divine purpose attached. For that reason, it is incumbent upon each one of us to find out what our purpose in life is.

Like God of purpose, we were created as beings of purpose:

And He has made from one blood every nation of men to dwell on all the face of the earth, and has determined their pre-appointed times and the boundaries of their dwellings, so that they should seek the Lord, in the hope that they might grope for Him and find Him, though He is not far from each one of us; for in Him we live and move and have our being, as also some of your own poets have said, "For we are also His offspring" (Acts 17:26-28).

Upon discovering one's purpose - joy, peace, fulfillment and happiness become synonymous and serve as a catalyst to accomplishment. Whatever God has entrusted to us; be it talents, gifts, abilities, calling and desires, it is ultimately for man's fulfillment and desires. You can only live the life you envision if you know and walk in purpose. In this pivotal work, The Joseph of Arimathea Calling, Dr. Francis Myles has cleverly exposed us to a generational truth that will change lives. I highly recommend this book to all leaders, believers, the marketplace, institutions of learning and those who are ready to shift to the next level."

~ HRM, King Adamtey I
(Dr. Kingsley Fletcher)
SUAPOLOR of the Se (Shai) Kingdom, Ghana
Global Leader, Motivational Speaker, Educator and Minister

Dr. Francis Myles' weighty message is relevant to the Body of Christ today, where many are grappling with the dilemma of how to unashamedly make money and still serve God whole-heartedly. His gift of grasping profound spiritual principles has earned him my respect.

Money is a powerful force. When money is married to the purpose of God, then it becomes a deadly weapon capable of plundering hell and populating heaven, so that the Kingdom of God is advanced.

In this life-changing book, Dr. Francis Myles has made the important connection between revelation and money. Every believer is responsible for seeking out revelation because you can only rise to the level of prosperity that you are equipped to handle. The way of the wealthy is quite simple – understand and live out specific principles. Dr. Francis Myles reminds us that the Bible is replete with life changing principles that God has hidden for us to search out, discover and apply. Only then shall our way become prosperous and we can have good success. Dr. Francis Myles has done the Body of Christ a great service by sharing the profound principles packed in the story of Joseph of Arimathea. This rich man's act of financing the agenda of God earned him his place in the Book of Life. Today God is looking for other 'Josephs of Arimathea' - believers who are not afraid to channel the wealth of the wicked into the house of God. This book is important for our times because it equips and deploys Christians to fulfil their calling beyond the pulpit and into the marketplace. God is looking for active participants and not just spectators of His end-time wealth transfer agenda. Let's heed this clarion call to impact this generation for Christ."

~ Neverl Kambasha, Chairman
Beryl Holdings
South Africa

Preface

ARE YOU AN END-TIME JOSEPH?

GOD IS RAISING an end-time company of Josephs across the nations of the world. This is a prophetic company of men and women who are bringing the fathering (mentoring) spirit to the marketplace. It is a "new breed" without greed. God is going to use this "Joseph Company" to generate billions of dollars in Kingdom resources. They will become what a friend of mine calls "Kingdom wealth masters!" It is a global network of ordinary men and women who are bringing the power of an extraordinary God into the corporate boardrooms and corridors of government! It is a network of Kingdom minded men and women who are using their God-given favor with their "Pharaoh" (business associates) to transform world systems into the Kingdoms of God and of His Christ.

This book is the study of one such "Joseph," Joseph of Arimathea to be specific. Joseph of Arimathea seemingly appears from nowhere to claim the lifeless body of Jesus. Who was this man? Why did God choose him for such an extraordinary Kingdom assignment? What does his life story teach us today about wealth creation and Kingdom entrepreneurship? These, plus many other questions are answered in this life-changing book. The book will also hopefully answer the questions below:

- Do you feel called to something FAR GREATER than what you are currently doing in the marketplace?
- Have you achieved great personal and business success yet still feel that there is something missing?
- Has God given you dreams for His Kingdom that cannot be contained within the four walls of the church?

It is my great honor and privilege to introduce you to the life of "Joseph of Arimathea." You will be pleasantly surprised by some of the wealth secrets of this mysterious disciple of Jesus. As you read, it will seem as though Joseph of Arimathea rose from the grave to tell his unfinished story.

Yours for Christ's Kingdom

Dr. Francis Myles
CEO: Francis Myles International
Senior Pastor: Royal Priesthood International Embassy
Tempe, Arizona

Kingdom Business Books – Vol 1

Table of Contents

1

THE TALE OF TWO JOSEPHS

THE TALE OF TWO JOSEPHS is an amazing fusion of two very intriguing marketplace and political personalities in the Bible. It's the tale of Joseph, the Prince of Egypt, the son of Jacob, in the Old Testament and of Joseph of Arimathea in the New Testament. What both of these larger than life historical figures have in common is the supernatural template for doing Kingdom business: acquiring wealth, managing wealth, and leveraging political influence in the marketplace in order to advance the Kingdom of God! This shared template between the two historic figures and how we can apply this same template to all Kingdom businessmen and women in the 21st-century is my primary motivation for writing this book.

My dear friend, Dr. Gordon Bradshaw, author of <u>I See Thrones</u>, recently launched a community transformational program called the 3M Project. The 3M Project represents the merging of the ministry, marketplace and municipality in order to transform a nation.

The purpose of the 3M Project is to create community based initiatives that are designed to bring practical solutions to the troubles of communities by engaging leaders in the church, marketplace and the municipality. Joseph of the Old Testament and Joseph of Arimathea in the New Testament are both living examples of the merging of three important streams of society; ministry, marketplace and municipality. Their lives provide us with working models on how to transform society for the greater good.

JOSEPH: THE LORD SHALL ADD!

So she called his name Joseph, and said, "The Lord shall add to me another son." Genesis 30:24

One of the most powerful spiritual technologies in Scripture is the technology of names. I wrote extensively about this ancient spiritual technology in The Order of Melchizedek; I humbly advise that you read this life-changing book. Names are so important in the spiritual realm; to such an extent that when God changed the name of "Jacob" to "Israel," the life and destiny of the man was forever altered (Genesis 32:24-26). I will quickly summarize the technology of names:

Names are…

1. Natures
2. Destinies
3. Dominions
4. Functions

God is very concerned about who names a person or an entity. The name of a thing informs us of its inherent nature, its appropriate destiny, the scope of its dominion, and the manner of its intended function. Armed with this understanding let us examine the first instance the name Joseph was used in Scripture. This usage of the name "Joseph" would enshrine the spiritual technology behind this name as it relates to the ongoing story of men and women advancing the Kingdom of God here on earth. In Hebrew, the meaning of the name Joseph is "May Jehovah add/give increase." This suggests "increase that is divinely inspired." Placed in the context of today's marketplace language we could say that the name Joseph means *increase or profits that are divinely inspired or fueled by the power of God.*

It is no wonder that Joseph is used by the Bible as the standard for emerging Kingdom entrepreneurs who desire to understand the inherent nature, scope and purpose of their God-given mantle for business. After many years of apostolic service to the Lord I have come to the sobering conclusion that there are many members of the Body of Christ who are truly anointed for business and others who definitely are not. The difference between the two is like day and night. This book is specifically written to people who are truly anointed for business. Nevertheless, this book includes some tools of wealth creation that affects people across the economic spectrum.

I'm convinced beyond a shadow of a doubt that we are about to see the global emergence of many Kingdom businessmen and women who will become end-time "Kingdom wealth masters." However, without working models for doing Kingdom business and without understanding the true purpose for wealth creation, many of these Kingdom wealth masters are at risk of being seduced by demonic powers that are prevalent in the marketplace. This will effectively minimize their Kingdom influence and tarnish their reputation.

By simply tracing the life of Joseph in the Old Testament we quickly discover that he truly lived up to the meaning of his name. Everywhere we see Joseph we also see supernatural addition or increase attending to everything he did. Everywhere he went, there was an increase in efficiencies, profits, human resources, systems and working capital. The following scriptural passages will attest to this Joseph phenomenon.

The name of a thing informs us of its inherent nature, its appropriate destiny, the scope of its dominion, and the manner of its intended function. The name Joseph suggests *increase that is divinely inspired.*

1. Potiphar's House

"The Lord was with Joseph, and he was a successful man; and he was in the house of his master the Egyptian. And his master saw that the Lord was with him and that the Lord made all he did to prosper in his hand. So Joseph found favor in his sight, and served him. Then he made him overseer of his house, and all that he had he put under his authority. So it was, from the time that he had made him overseer of his house and all that he had, that the Lord blessed the Egyptian's house for Joseph's sake; and the blessing of the Lord was on all that he had in the house and in the field. Thus he left all that he had in Joseph's hand, and he did not know what he had except for the bread, which he ate. Now Joseph was handsome in form and appearance." Genesis 39:2-6

2. In The Jail House

"Then Joseph's master took him and put him into the prison, a place where the king's prisoners were confined. And he was there in the prison. But the Lord was with Joseph and showed him mercy, and He gave him favor in the sight of the keeper of the prison. And the keeper of the prison committed to Joseph's hand all the prisoners who were in the prison; whatever they did there, it was his doing. The keeper of the prison did not look into anything that was under Joseph's authority, because the Lord was with him; and whatever he did, the Lord made it prosper." Genesis 39:20-23

3. In Pharaoh's Palace

"Now therefore, let Pharaoh select a discerning and wise man, and set him over the land of Egypt. Let Pharaoh do this, and let him appoint officers over the land, to collect one-fifth of the produce of the land of Egypt in the seven plentiful years. And let them gather all the food of those good years that are coming, and store up grain under the authority of Pharaoh, and let them keep food in the cities. Then that food shall be as a reserve for the land for the seven years of famine which shall be in the land of Egypt, that the land may not perish during the famine." So the advice was good in the eyes of Pharaoh and in the eyes of all his servants. And Pharaoh said to his servants, "Can we find such a one as this, a man in whom is the Spirit of God?" Then Pharaoh said to Joseph, "Inasmuch as God has shown you all this, there is no one as discerning and wise as you. You shall be over my house, and all my people shall be ruled according to your word; only in regard to the throne will I be greater than you." And Pharaoh said to Joseph, "See, I have set you over all the land of Egypt." Then Pharaoh took his signet ring off his hand and put it on Joseph's hand; and he clothed him in garments of fine linen and put a gold chain around his neck. And he had him ride in the second chariot, which he had; and they cried out before him, "Bow the knee!" So he set him over all the land of Egypt." Genesis 41:33-43

JOSEPH: THE COAT OF MANY COLORS

Now Israel loved Joseph more than all his children, because he was the son of his old age. Also, he made him a tunic of many colors. But when his brothers saw that their father loved him more than all his brothers, they hated him and could not speak peaceably to him. Genesis 37:3-4

Anyone who has a calling to be a "Joseph" e.g. Kingdom entrepreneur, needs to understand the responsibility that accompanies this mantle, this "coat of many colors!" God is the one who gives this precious mantle to individuals He has called to be Kingdom wealth masters for the purpose of advancing His Kingdom. Nevertheless, it is important to remember that the coat of many colors also attracts the jealousies of those who do not have it. If you know you carry the coat of many colors in the spirit realm you must be thick skinned against unwarranted criticisms that will come from those who can't understand why you are so rich and highly favored and they are not. Even in the Body of Christ having the coat of many colors does not guarantee that everyone in the church will accept or respect your calling.

The million-dollar question that we need to answer is simply this: "Why does God grant men and women with a "Joseph Calling" the coat of many colors?" Please remember that God is motivated solely by purpose. Purpose is the divine intent behind the creation of a thing. In my time of prayer and Bible study the Lord showed me that there are four main reasons the "coat of many colors" is needed by

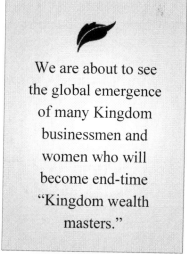

We are about to see the global emergence of many Kingdom businessmen and women who will become end-time "Kingdom wealth masters."

men and women who are called to be Kingdom entrepreneurs. Namely:

- The "coat of many colors" represents the ability to do Kingdom business across racial, ethnic, cultural, and national divides. The train of commerce will come to a screeching halt if a Kingdom entrepreneur's business model does not allow him or her to break through these barriers. One of the reasons Apple and Facebook are multi-billion dollar companies is because their business models and products were specifically designed to break through racial, ethnic, cultural and national divides in order to acquire and service millions of customers.

- The "coat of many colors" represents God's supernatural favor that causes Kingdom entrepreneurs to conduct successful business ventures across multiple industries and geographical boundaries. Business people who cannot conduct commerce across multiple industries and geographical borders (state and national) will be limited in their ability to amass great wealth for the cause of Christ. Donald Trump is a multi-billionaire real estate mogul because he has mastered "the art of the deal" across multiple industries as well as state and international borders.

- The "coat of many colors" represents the supernatural ability to multi-task across multiple projects and even multiple businesses for the purpose of manifesting increase in one's storehouse for the advancement of the Kingdom of God. We see this unique ability in Joseph as he managed the worst global economic crisis while also administrating the many affairs of the country during his tenure as prime minister of Egypt.

- The "coat of many colors" represents the special affinity that God has for people who "favor" His righteous cause. Awarding the "coat of many colors" is God's way of "delighting in the prosperity of His servants" (Psalm 35:27).

JOSEPH: DREAMS OF GREATNESS!

Now Joseph had a dream, and he told it to his brothers; and they hated him even more. So he said to them, "Please hear this dream which I have dreamed: There we were, binding sheaves in the field. Then behold, my sheaf arose and also stood upright; and indeed your sheaves stood all around and bowed down to my sheaf." And his brothers said to him, "Shall you indeed reign over us? Or shall you indeed have dominion over us?" So they hated him even more for his dreams and for his words. Genesis 37:5-8

Every man or woman that I have ever met who carries the "Joseph Calling" is pregnant with dreams of inspired greatness. The desire to achieve greatness is deeply embedded in the spiritual DNA of every person who is called to be a "Kingdom paymaster" (Kingdom paymasters are people who know that they exist solely to fund the gospel of the Kingdom). In observing high achievers in

9

different disciplines across four continents I have come to the sobering conclusion that greatness cannot be achieved if the person doesn't think it is possible for him or her. When it comes to manifesting extraordinary levels of achievement, visualizing or dreaming about becoming great is a necessary ingredient in the process of becoming. I once heard the renowned motivational speaker, Les Brown, say, "if you think you can, you can but if you think you can't you are right too." The point being made here is that no one can achieve lasting success above his or her level of thinking. King Solomon says it this way, "whatever a man thinks, so is he!" (Proverbs 23:7)

What is worth noting is the response of Joseph's brothers to his dream of greatness. Joseph's brothers did not applaud their younger brother for thinking-outside-the-box. They were definitely not happy that greatness was even possible in the life of their younger sibling. Instead of celebrating him, Joseph's dreams of greatness infuriated them and engineered their hatred of him. The real sobering question is "Why?" The answer is simple but worth noting for every person who carries the "Joseph Calling:" your passion for greatness scares those who are terrified of thinking-outside-the-box. When people

God is motivated solely by purpose. Purpose is the divine intent behind the creation of a thing.

you thought would support your dreams of greatness attack you instead, don't take it personally.

Most people are afraid of their own shadows let alone the dreams of greatness of another. Notwithstanding, every "Joseph" (Kingdom entrepreneur) that I have met is not afraid of being rich or becoming great, nor are they afraid of greatness. Almost all high achievers hate mediocrity and are not afraid to swim in shark-infested waters to manifest the dreams that God gave them. I have a question for you. "How BIG are your Dreams?" I am a firm believer that the size of your dreams will determine the size of your God.

PIMPS, PROSTITUTES & MISTRESSES!

Now Joseph was handsome in form and appearance. And it came to pass after these things that his master's wife cast longing eyes on Joseph, and she said, "Lie with me." But he refused and said to his master's wife, "Look, my master does not know what is with me in the house, and he has committed all that he has to my hand. There is no one greater in this house than I, nor has he kept back anything from me but you, because you are his wife. How then can I do this great wickedness, and sin against God?" So it was, as she spoke to Joseph day by day, that he did not heed her, to lie with her or to be with her. Genesis 39:7-10

Since I am entitled to my opinion, I will just go ahead and say it: The greatest threats to men and women in the Kingdom of God who are called to be high achievers are "pimps, prostitutes and mistresses." Most high achievers, especially men, have fallen into financial ruin because of wrong associations with the opposite sex. Without a doubt one of the most powerful natural instincts is the desire for sex. I recently heard Jim Evans, founder of "Marriage Today" say, "men don't want sex, they NEED sex!" This is how God wired them from the beginning of time because they are the life givers. Regrettably, since the fall of man, man's sexual drive has become intensely perverted.

Visualizing or dreaming about becoming great is a necessary ingredient in the process of becoming.

Every highly successful person in the Kingdom of God needs to watch out for what Bishop TD Jakes calls the "seductive power of PMS: Power, Money and Sex." Many rich and successful people have been destroyed by one of these three vices with sex topping the list for many male Kingdom entrepreneurs. Nothing can attract the opposite sex like money. This is why the corporate world is plagued with extra-marital sexual affairs between leaders of corporations and those looking to ascend the illustrious corporate ladder of success. As more women have added their names to the elite list of some of the world's most wealthy persons, there has been a growing trend of men who marry women solely for the purpose of exploiting them for money. In the name of love these street pimps are running away with the bank, after crushing the heart of a woman who thought he married her for love and not for her money.

The world's oldest profession, prostitution has benefited greatly from the sexual indulgences of the world's wealthy. Unfortunately, the list of wealthy people seeking the services of prostitutes also includes many so-called Christian businessmen and sometimes women. The point I am trying to drive home is simply this: every person with a Joseph calling will be tested in the area of sexual promiscuity. I pray to God that you will pass the test with flying colors like Joseph of old. When Joseph's inherent ability to manage and grow businesses brought him into a place of prominence in Potiphar's house, he had to fight against serious sexual advances from Potiphar's wife. While Potiphar was at work in pharaoh's palace his wife was working tirelessly to seduce Joseph. She had one clear obsession; she wanted to have sex with Joseph at all costs. Joseph knew that this action would violate his kingly and priestly mantle as well as damage his personal relationship with God so he never succumbed to the temptation. There is a demonic principality that targets rich and successful people for illicit sexual affairs, including addiction to pornography. It's my prayer that the Lord will deliver every "mover and shaker" in His Kingdom who is reading this book from the spirit of sexual perversion and promiscuity.

JOSEPH: WISE WEALTH MANAGER

Joseph was thirty years old when he stood before Pharaoh king of Egypt. And Joseph went out from the presence of Pharaoh, and went throughout all the land of Egypt. Now in the seven plentiful years the ground brought forth abundantly. So he gathered up all the food of the seven years, which were in the land of Egypt, and laid up the food in the cities; he laid up in every city the food of the fields which surrounded them. Joseph gathered very much grain, as the sand of the sea, until he stopped counting, for it was immeasurable. Genesis 41:46-49

The world is in dire need of faithful, wise and highly gifted wealth managers. It's a shame if the above caliber of wealth managers does not emerge from among God's people. God is releasing end-time wealth for the purpose of advancing His Kingdom on a scale the world has never seen before. Many of God's people are going to receive a supernatural wealth transfer but managing a lot of money is easier said than done. I have always told my audience that knowing how to steward and manage a blessing is more important than receiving it. I have heard that many people who win large sums of money in a lottery are broke within five years! Why? Money will test and expose every flaw in a person's character that will eventually become his or her undoing. There is a very powerful emotion that is attached to having a lot of money that defeats the best intentions of most people who come into a lot of money suddenly. Nevertheless, the fact remains that the church is about to experience the greatest transfer of wealth the Body of Christ has ever known. The church's new millionaires and billionaires will need "Josephs" who are faithful, trustworthy, and gifted at managing large sums of money.

Pharaoh took one look at Joseph, listened to his brilliant proposal about how to manage the seven years of plenty and safeguard the national economy during the seven years of famine and knew instantly that there was no better wealth manager in the whole of Egypt than the thirty-year-old Jewish man who was standing in front of him. He quickly appointed him to the second highest political position in Egypt: prime minister. He made Joseph prime minister of Egypt answerable only to himself (Pharaoh). Joseph immediately created a system of savings that had

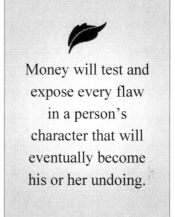

Money will test and expose every flaw in a person's character that will eventually become his or her undoing.

not been practiced before. He commissioned the building of large granaries and calculated that a saving of twenty percent of Egypt's gross domestic product (GDP) was more than sufficient to sustain the nation during the seven years of famine. Joseph was such a good and gifted manager that by the time the famine ended, Pharaoh was richer than before the famine began. This is the same kind of wealth master God wants to raise in the Body of Christ.

JOSEPH: TRADING FUTURES

Now therefore, let Pharaoh select a discerning and wise man, and set him over the land of Egypt. Let Pharaoh do this, and let him appoint officers over the land, to collect one-fifth of the produce of the land of Egypt in the seven plentiful years. And let them gather all the food of those good years that are coming, and store up grain under the authority of Pharaoh, and let them keep food in the cities. Then that food shall be as a reserve for the land for the seven years of famine which shall be in the land of Egypt, that the land may not perish during the famine. Genesis 39:33-36

One of the most fascinating aspects of trading on the New York Stock Exchange and many other internationally recognized stock exchanges is called "futures trading." Billions of dollars are made each day trading futures but as the term also suggests many speculative investors have also lost fortunes when "trade winds" went against them. Futures trading is one of the most speculative aspects of trading on any stock exchange. Traders have literally traded away their future earnings with one bad futures trade.

Long before Wall Street discovered futures trading, Joseph was trading for the future through his prophetic anointing and stellar business acumen. He created a business and trading strategy that hedged present earnings in Egypt against future losses through a severe famine that was yet to come. This famine would lead to the worst global economic recession of the ancient world. Had Joseph

16

not effectively traded futures Egypt and every other nation would have been wiped off the face of the earth by the ensuing famine.

Kingdom entrepreneurs must ask the Holy Spirit to anoint them with this uncanny prophetic ability to discern tomorrow's business climate and how it will affect them. Business leaders who consume all of their company's profits in the same year that they are earned are not wise. They are definitely not trading for the future. Joseph developed a business plan that compelled every industry in Egypt to save 20% of everything that was produced in Egypt. In America "insider trading" is illegal, because you are trading a stock while knowing its future performance. Martha Stewart, a very famous American TV personality, food baron, and businesswoman went to jail for six months for insider trading. However, in God's Kingdom, insider trading is perfectly legal. The Holy Spirit is capable of showing Kingdom entrepreneurs "things yet to come!" This means that the Holy Ghost is able to show you a stock to buy before that stock is even profitable for purchase, whether it is in a bear or bull market.

JOSEPH: THE POWER OF FORGIVENESS

Thus you shall say to Joseph: "I beg you, please forgive the trespass of your brothers and their sin; for they did evil to you."' Now, please, forgive the trespass of the servants of the God of your father." And Joseph wept when they spoke to him. Then his brothers also went and fell down before his face, and they said, "Behold, we are your servants." Joseph said to them, "Do not be afraid, for am I in the place of God? But as for you, you meant evil against me; but God meant it for good, in order to bring it about as it is this day, to save many people alive. Now therefore, do not be afraid; I will provide for you and your little ones." And he comforted them and spoke kindly to them. Genesis 50:17-21

Many of the intrinsic qualities of Joseph are very impressive to say the least. Notwithstanding, there is no intrinsic quality about Joseph that impresses me more than his ability to forgive. I believe that the area of forgiveness is a critical arena in the lives of many Kingdom entrepreneurs. The reason for this is obvious; man is inherently flawed. Consequently, the chances of being hurt or betrayed by people, especially in the marketplace, are quite high. I believe that unforgiveness is the reason many women and men in the Kingdom of God who are called to function in the "Joseph Calling" never realize their full potential in Christ. In the free market system, it is possible for promising business ventures to fail; even when Kingdom citizens, doing business together, have the best of intentions. It is very common for partners of a failed business venture to part ways in anger and bitterness because the business failed. In addition to the emotions of anger and bitterness, each partner often blames the other for the demise of the business. When God's people are involved in a failed business venture the ensuing emotional tension can be quite detrimental to maintaining the *unity of the Spirit in the bond of peace* (Ephesians 4:1-2).

If anybody was justified in staying angry it was Joseph. He was violently betrayed by his own brothers who were supposed to be his greatest protectors. Instead of protecting him, Joseph's older brothers felt they were justified in selling him as a slave to the Ishmaelite's (Genesis 37:25-28). Only God knows how traumatic Joseph's journey to Egypt was under the care of the Ishmaelite slave traders. Slave traders were never known for their generosity or kindness towards their captives. In almost every instance they were extremely cruel taskmasters to their cargo of slaves. Joseph was most likely beaten, even tortured on the difficult journey to Egypt. Who would have blamed him for being bitter towards his brothers?

> Kingdom entrepreneurs must ask the Holy Spirit to anoint them with this uncanny prophetic ability to discern tomorrow's climate and how it will affect them.

I would not have blamed Joseph for seeking vengeance when his ill-willed brothers came strolling into Egypt begging for bread. It was certainly within his political power to seek immediate retribution for wrongs done to him by his brothers. Instead of vengeance, supernatural compassion for his brothers welled up in Joseph's heart. He had forgiven them long before they showed up on the shores of

Egypt. When Jacob died, Joseph's brothers were once again overcome by guilt and fear of retribution for what they had done to him. They came to Joseph and bowed before him to beg for his forgiveness. However, there was no need to fear because revenge was the furthest thing from Joseph's mind. What Joseph told his brothers then is worth repeating here, because this is the object lesson every "Joseph" (Kingdom entrepreneur) must understand about life's difficult challenges: *"But as for you, you meant evil against me; but God meant it for good, in order to bring it about as it is this day, to save many people alive"* (Genesis 50:20). Every Kingdom entrepreneur must know that God can turn what their enemies meant for evil to their good. This is why there is no reason to hold on to grudges that poison the soul with the dreaded root of bitterness and unforgiveness.

JOSEPH: FORGING STRATEGIC POLITICAL ALLIANCES

Then Pharaoh took his signet ring off his hand and put it on Joseph's hand; and he clothed him in garments of fine linen and put a gold chain around his neck. And he had him ride in the second chariot which he had; and they cried out before him, "Bow the knee!" So he set him over all the land of Egypt. Pharaoh also said to Joseph, "I am Pharaoh, and without your consent no man may lift his hand or foot in all the land of Egypt." And Pharaoh called Joseph's name Zaphnath-

Paaneah. And he gave him as a wife Asenath, the daughter of Poti-Pherah priest of On. So Joseph went out over all the land of Egypt. Genesis 41:42-45

We live in a world that revolves around, and is heavily controlled by, politics; making politicians key players in any meaningful societal engagement. In most nations politicians are also called "lawmakers or legislators." This is because many of their political policies can be transformed into criminal and civil laws that impact every area of society and commerce. The world of politics is no longer a domain in which God's people can refuse to participate. We can no longer excuse ourselves from actively engaging the political domain by simply saying, "Politics is a dirty game." Well, I have news for you: that so-called "dirty game" will affect most of your business and individual aspirations, including your right to worship freely. In some nations, attracting investors into the economy is very difficult because of a very hostile political environment that has literally crippled the marketplace. Additionally, politicians are more often than not, the leaders of government in almost every nation on earth. They literally run the institution of human government whose tentacles literally affect every area of societal engagement. This would explain why God took Daniel into the courts of Babylon.

I never really saw Joseph of the Old Testament as a politician. I always viewed him through the lenses of a prophet and Kingdom businessman but the Lord showed me that Joseph became a politician the moment he accepted Pharaoh's offer to become Egypt's prime minister. Joseph also entered into a politically arranged marriage when he married the daughter of the Priest of Oni at Pharaoh's request. Joseph's dual ability to engage the business marketplace as well as the political arena is the reason he was so successful in reforming Egypt. Kingdom entrepreneurs must prepare themselves to forge strategic political alliances across the nations in order to advance both the Kingdom and their business

Every Kingdom entrepreneur must know that God can turn what their enemies meant for evil to their good. This is why there is no reason to hold on to grudges that poison the soul with the dreaded root of bitterness and unforgiveness.

interests. We will see in a later chapter that it is clear Joseph of Arimathea had done exactly that; forged a strong and strategic political alliance with Pontus Pilate (Governor of Rome). We will see how he could leverage that relationship at a very critical time in human history.

JOSEPH: PHARAOH,
AND THE EGYPTIAN MARKETPLACE

And Joseph gathered up all the money that was found in the land of Egypt and in the land of Canaan, for the grain, which they bought; and Joseph brought the money into Pharaoh's house. So when the money failed in the land of Egypt and in the land of Canaan, all the Egyptians came to Joseph and said, "Give us bread, for why should we die in your presence? For the money has failed." Genesis 47:14-15

In recent years, there has been a lot of talk in the global church about the "Joseph anointing." I have met several godly businessmen and women who believe that God has called them to be a "Joseph to their generation." This is truly exciting because Joseph is a biblical prototype of how a Kingdom businessperson is supposed to operate in the marketplace and in the political arena. Unfortunately, many

We can no longer excuse ourselves from actively engaging the political domain by simply saying "Politics is a dirty game."

pastors and businesspersons who are excited about the return of the Joseph anointing to the church and marketplace, do not fully understand what this really means.

To understand who Joseph was in the scope of God's Kingdom economy, we must ask ourselves several key questions. I will ask them here but I will answer them fully in Chapter Three.

1. What priestly Order was Joseph operating under when he was in Egypt?
2. Why did God give Joseph incredible favor with Pharaoh?
3. What position did Joseph hold in Egypt?
4. Why did God give Joseph such massive global influence?
5. Why is God raising a corporate Joseph in the earth today?

JOSEPH OF ARIMATHEA

Now when evening had come, there came a rich man from Arimathea, named Joseph, who himself had also become a disciple of Jesus. Matthew 27:57

While I am mesmerized by the life, business, and political acumen of Joseph of the Old Testament, I was completely stunned by the astounding revelation that the Holy Spirit exploded in my spirit recently. This revelation came to me while I was getting ready to minister to a group of businessmen and political leaders in George, South Africa. It's safe to say that this revelation has changed the projectile of my ministry to business leaders in the Kingdom of God. It also precipitated the writing of the book that you are now holding in your hands.

Here is the revelation that I received: the LORD showed me that Joseph of Arimathea is the apex of the kind of Kingdom entrepreneur that God desires to use as the end of this "age of sin" rapidly approaches. In short order, Joseph of Arimathea is the consummation of the Joseph calling that began with Joseph of the Old Testament. Joseph of Arimathea is the kind of rich man every Kingdom entrepreneur must aspire to become. The Holy Spirit showed me that Joseph of Arimathea represents a higher Kingdom model for Kingdom entrepreneurship and the true purpose of wealth than Joseph of the Old Testament.

I was speechless, after the LORD told me this. How could a man who is only mentioned in three to four verses of Scripture be the bearer of the highest standard for Kingdom entrepreneurship that all Kingdom entrepreneurs must aspire to? "What is it about this man that holds the key to the true purpose of wealth in the Kingdom of God?" These and other questions flooded my mind; but the answers left me teary eyed. As the Holy Spirit flooded my spirit and soul with revelation about Joseph of Arimathea I was moved deeply in my spirit. It was as though Joseph of Arimathea rose from the grave to tell me his story. A story that would forever change how I saw wealthy disciples of Christ! When he was finished telling it; scales of ignorance fell from my eyes. I found myself saying, "Wow!!!" Why didn't I see this before in all my reading of the account of Joseph of Arimathea in the gospels? I believe your reaction will be just as powerful as mine.

DOES GOD WANT ME TO BE WEALTHY?

ONE OF THE MOST consequential questions we could ever ask ourselves is the question, "Does God want me to be wealthy?" This is truly one of the most important questions that Kingdom entrepreneurs and people who sense a strong calling from God to be Kingdom wealth masters need to answer effectively. There can be no gray areas in how we answer this question, especially from a theological perspective. It's quite difficult to exercise faith for finances if we are not sure about God's will concerning becoming wealthy in His Kingdom. The Bible is quite clear that the *"Just shall live by faith,"* (Hebrews 10:38) but faith is impossible to attain where the will of God is not known. This is because *"faith comes by hearing and hearing by the Word of God"* (Romans 10:17). This is why it's my humble opinion that this chapter is one of the most important chapters in this entire book. It is my goal in this chapter to make it absolutely clear that becoming wealthy is within the framework of God's will for all His dear children.

IS IT DIFFICULT FOR RICH PEOPLE TO ENTER HEAVEN?

And again I say to you, it is easier for a camel to go through the eye of a needle than for a rich man to enter the kingdom of God." When His disciples heard it, they were greatly astonished, saying, "Who then can be saved?" But Jesus looked at them and said to them, "With men this is impossible, but with God all things are possible." Matthew 19:24-26

Perhaps there is no other scripture that has been used by religious people to heap tremendous guilt on wealthy members of the Body of Christ as the above passage of scripture. The first time I heard a pastor teach on this scripture I instantly became terrified of becoming wealthy! I was left with the impression that wealth was to be avoided like the common plague even though my personal experience had more than proved to me that being poor was one of the most demeaning experiences a human being can ever go through. Notwithstanding, after listening to this pastor preach with great passion about the danger of being wealthy I was mortified to say the least. In his teaching, the pastor made it quite clear that becoming super-rich can sentence a human being to an eternity in hell's fires. God knew that my deepest desire was to go to heaven and live with Him forever. I had always set heaven in my sights after the demise of my life here on earth; I certainly had no intentions of going to hell. If becoming wealthy in God's kingdom was also synonymous with going to hell I wanted no part of it.

Fortunately for all of us, the passage quoted above is not a divine repudiation of the wealthy or super-rich. If this passage was such a rejection of those with great wealth it would fly in the face of biblical history and precedence. Many of the Patriarchs in the Bible such as Abraham, Isaac and Jacob, where all super wealthy. Joseph, in his lofty position as Prime Minister of Egypt would qualify in today's economy as a multi-billionaire. Does this mean that Abraham, Isaac and Jacob are now burning in the fiery flames of hell because they were super wealthy when they were alive? One of the challenges in interpreting

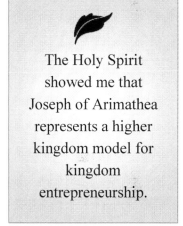

The Holy Spirit showed me that Joseph of Arimathea represents a higher kingdom model for kingdom entrepreneurship.

Scripture is understanding the fact that the Bible is not a Gentile book, it's a Jewish book. Without understanding prevailing Jewish culture, idioms and customs the Bible was written in, it's quite difficult to properly interpret Scripture in its proper context. The Lord Jesus Christ was a master at using allegory to teach deeper spiritual truths about how His Kingdom operates.

Let us now examine Matthew 19:24-26 thoroughly and see what Jesus is really saying. *"And again I say to you, it is easier for a camel to go through the eye of a needle than for a rich man to enter the Kingdom of God."* In Jewish tradition, the eye of a needle was a small gate entrance into the city of Jerusalem. This gate was so small that when merchants came with their cargo on the backs of camels, the only way their precious cargo could be brought into the city was to have their camels slouch to the ground and enter the "eye of the needle" on their knees. Slouching on one's knees in order to enter a gateway is a prophetic symbol of the kind of humility God expects in people who want to enter His Kingdom. It is quite clear from Scripture that *"God resists the proud and gives grace to the humble"* (James 5:6-7). There are a lot of people who were very poor on earth, who died and went to hell. Without a doubt, wealth did not play any part in putting them there.

The expression "to enter the kingdom of God" in the above scriptural passage is not a reference about going to heaven. It is not even a reference about going to hell. The expression in the text "to enter the kingdom of God" refers to God's way of doing things. In other words, Jesus is saying it is quite difficult for rich people to enter into God's way of doing things if they are not willing to "humble themselves," i.e., enter the Kingdom of God by kneeling through the eye of the needle (gateway). Suddenly the text becomes abundantly clear, Jesus is not repudiating being wealthy. To the contrary, Jesus was warning the rich in His Kingdom to watch for the cancer of self-dependence that having money can produce in the soul. The fall of man produced the cancer of self-dependence inside man's soul that makes him want to depend on his own efforts instead of depending on God. Jesus is essentially telling us that having lots of money only increases our capacity to depend on ourselves rather than depend on God.

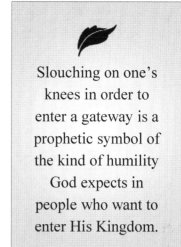

Slouching on one's knees in order to enter a gateway is a prophetic symbol of the kind of humility God expects in people who want to enter His Kingdom.

When His disciples heard it, they were greatly astonished, saying, "Who then can be saved?" The disciples' response to what Jesus said demonstrates that they failed to understand the allegory Jesus was using to warn those who are wealthy against falling for the "deceitfulness of riches." (Mark 4:19). They took His statement as a clear repudiation of being wealthy and they were petrified by the eternal implications of what they thought Jesus was saying. They probably knew of loved ones who fit the description of being rich or super-wealthy. Were their loved ones going to go to hell just because they were rich? This is a scary thought anyway you twist it. Therefore, the disciples declared in utter dismay, "Who then can be saved?" Their question and sense of desperation suggests that they knew many people that fit the description of being rich, and thus would be excluded from entering the Kingdom of God. Thankfully, they were wrong. They had misunderstood Jesus' whole point. The matter Jesus was addressing was not being rich but the need for humility in order to enter the Kingdom of God.

Thankfully, Jesus looked at them and said to them, *"With men this is impossible, but with God all things are possible."* Jesus' response to ease His disciples' dismay underscores the fact that He knew that they totally misunderstood Him and the context of His allegory. Since His subject matter was about the need for humility and not about being rich, Jesus plainly declares, "With men this is impossible!" What is impossible with men? Humility! Humility is impossible for fallen man to manifest, because pride or self-independence lies at the core of all fallen descendants of Adam. Jesus then declares, "but with God all things are possible." What is possible with God? It is possible to be rich and yet walk in complete heartfelt humility before God, who is the true source of our wealth. When the Lord, revealed this to me all the fears that I held inside my soul about being rich disappeared. I now know for a fact that I can be rich and still walk humbly before my God just like Abraham, Isaac and Jacob.

PROSPERITY GOSPEL OR
THE GOSPEL OF THE KINGDOM?

Now if God so clothes the grass of the field, which today is, and tomorrow is thrown into the oven, will He not much more clothe you, O you of little faith? "Therefore do not worry, saying, 'What shall we eat?' or 'What shall we drink?' or

'What shall we wear?' For after all these things the Gentiles seek. For your heavenly Father knows that you need all these things. But seek first the kingdom of God and His righteousness, and all these things shall be added to you. Matthew 6:30-33

In recent years, there's been a lot of talk about the prosperity gospel. Much of the talk on social media about the prosperity gospel is heavily negative. Many Christians see the prosperity gospel as a misrepresentation of the gospel of Jesus Christ by greedy preachers. On the other hand, you have serious proponents of the prosperity gospel who can clearly demonstrate how being rich has enabled them to advance the gospel of Jesus Christ. They are convinced that being poor would never have afforded them the same opportunities to speak for the cause of Christ. They quickly point to the millions of people who have been saved through the preaching of the gospel through the expensive medium of television as one of the many benefits of being rich.

> Humility is impossible for fallen man to manifest, because pride or self-independence lies at the core of all fallen descendants of Adam but Jesus declares, "with God all things are possible."

Unfortunately for them, some of the key proponents of the prosperity gospel have brought tremendous disrepute to the Body of Christ. For some, the prosperity gospel became nothing short of a cloak of covetousness and unbridled materialism. Their excesses impeach the true spirit of the Gospel of Jesus Christ. However, there is always the danger of "throwing out the baby with the bath water!" Several "bad apples among the bunch" does not necessarily mean that every preacher or person who believes in the prosperity gospel is driven by greed.

Nevertheless, the whole talk about the prosperity gospel misses the larger point; Jesus never talked about the prosperity gospel. You'll be very hard pressed to find a message in the gospels that Jesus preached about the prosperity gospel. The reason is staggeringly simple; prosperity in itself is not a gospel but it is part and parcel of a larger body of thought, "the Gospel of the Kingdom!" The reason Jesus never talked about the prosperity gospel is because there was no need to. Jesus always assumed that financial and material prosperity are an integral part of the Gospel of the Kingdom. If you examine the Bible in its entirety, a serious case for the gospel of prosperity can be mounted easily. However, since the whole Bible is about the restoration of the Kingdom, the subject of prosperity is better handled from within the perspective of restoring the Kingdom of God. At the end of this chapter I will introduce you to the Kingdom concept of "Commonwealth." Understanding this Kingdom concept will eliminate any misgivings you may have about becoming rich or super-wealthy in God's Kingdom. Understanding the Kingdom concept of commonwealth, will completely put to rest the question, "Does God want me to be wealthy?"

IS THERE NOT A CAUSE?

Now Eliab his oldest brother heard when he spoke to the men; and Eliab's anger was aroused against David, and he said, "Why did you come down here? And with whom have you left those few sheep in the wilderness? I know your pride and the insolence of your heart, for you have come down to see the battle." And David said, "What have I done now? Is there not a cause?" 1 Samuel 17:28-29

One of the biblical stories that can shed some light on the question that we are grappling with (does God want you to be wealthy?) is the story of David and Goliath. For forty-days Goliath, the Philistine giant, was taunting the armies of Israel to send one man to fight him in a "winner takes all death match." None of the men in the Israeli army volunteered to take on the daunting challenge. Instead, the entire army was petrified of the monstrous giant in front of them. David happened to walk onto the battlefield at the exact moment when Goliath was again taunting the armies of Israel. David was so infuriated by the arrogance in the voice of the Philistine giant that he began to ask the men in the army what would be done for the man who slew the giant on behalf of the people of God.

When Eliab, David's older brother discovered what David was about to do, he was infuriated. He accused David of being full of arrogance. David wisely responded, "What have I done now? Is there not a cause?" I believe David's answer is a fitting answer to the question, "Does God want me to be wealthy?" The real question we

35

need to ask ourselves is, "Is there not a cause" in the Kingdom that requires us to be wealthy in order to achieve it?

> *Let them shout for joy and be glad, Who favor my righteous cause. And let them say continually, Let the Lord be magnified. Who has pleasure in the prosperity of His servant.*
> Psalm 35:27

Listen to what David says in the above Psalm. "Let them shout for joy and be glad." Who does "them" in the text stand for? Who is he referring to? He gives us the answer in the very next part of the verse. "Them" is people "Who favor my righteous cause." Remember, Jesus taught us that when we seek His Kingdom and His righteousness, "all of these things (financial and material things) would be added to our portfolio" (Matthew 6:33 KJV, paraphrased). In other words, when we are seeking His Kingdom and righteousness above all other things, "we favor His righteous cause." It's very clear from reading the four Gospels that Jesus' number one mission on earth was to restore the Kingdom and its righteous standards of living. This was absolutely His "righteous cause" and still is!

King David continues the Psalm by declaring *"And let them say continually, "Let the Lord be magnified."* Why? The last part of the verse makes it known: *"Who has pleasure in the prosperity of His servant."* Wow! Do you mean to tell me that God actually takes tremendous pleasure in the "prosperity of His servant?" Absolutely! Not only are we His servants in the propagation of the Gospel of Jesus

Christ, which is the Gospel of the Kingdom, we are sons of God also. The Scripture is clear that *"this Gospel of the Kingdom will and must be preached before the end of this present age of sin and darkness can come."* (Matthew 24 KJV, paraphrased). Glory to God in the highest! I want you to notice what is missing in the Psalm: the expression, "and God delights in the poverty of His servant." The reason is obvious. Poverty is a curse and its presence in the life of a child of God does not please the Holy Spirit. To the contrary it grieves the Holy Spirit when God's children live below their God given ambassadorial, aristocrat rights and privileges. If there was ever a "cause" for God's children to be wealthy, none can be greater than the need to advance the Kingdom and preach Jesus to all the nations!

KING SOLOMON:
THE RICHEST MAN WHO EVER LIVED!

*Then God said to Solomon: "Because this was in your heart, and you have not asked riches or wealth or honor or the life of your enemies, nor have you asked long life—but have asked wisdom and knowledge for yourself, that you may judge My people over whom I have made you king— wisdom and knowledge are granted to you; and I will give you riches and wealth and honor, such as none of the kings have had who were before you, nor shall any after you have the like."*2 Chronicles 1:11-12

No one can dispute what is now an established historical fact, that King Solomon was the richest and wisest man who has ever lived. What makes the life of King Solomon so interesting is that Solomon did not start out wanting to be the richest and the wisest man who has ever lived. He became the king of Israel at the tender age of twelve years old. I can imagine that becoming the king of a great nation at the tender age of twelve would be a daunting task for anybody. It was no different for the young King Solomon.

While King Solomon was sleeping, God appeared to him in a dream. In the dream the Lord asked him to name whatever he wanted to receive from God. Literally speaking, God was giving the young king the opportunity to write the ticket of his own destiny. Instead of asking for wealth and riches or the life of his enemies, never mind long life for himself, King Solomon asked for divine wisdom. He asked God to give him a wise and discerning heart so he could judge God's people (the Israelites) in righteousness. Apparently, God was very impressed with Solomon's request. God told Solomon in the dream that since he did not ask for wealth and riches or for the life of his enemies; God promised to give him honor, riches and wealth like none of the kings before him or thereafter. History has more than proven that God kept His promise to King Solomon. Up to the present day they have never been a person, dead or alive who has managed to surpass King Solomon's wealth and riches or his wisdom (as of September 30, 2016 the Bloomberg Billionaire daily index shows that Bill Gates is worth $89 Billion; however, that still falls short of King Solomon's estimated net worth of over $100 Billion[1]).

Nevertheless, it's this statement in the text that caught my attention, *"and I will give you riches and wealth and honor, such as none of the kings have had who were before you, nor shall any after you have the like."* Do you mean to tell me that it was actually God and not man who gave King Solomon riches and wealth beyond that of any king who has ever lived? The answer is absolutely yes! God was the source of King Solomon's untold riches and wealth. If such is the case, why are we still grappling with the question "Does God want me to be wealthy?" If being super-wealthy sentences a person to a lifetime in hell's fires why would God tempt King Solomon with such poison? It would seem like it would be more honorable for God to make King Solomon the poorest king who has

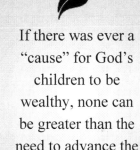

If there was ever a "cause" for God's children to be wealthy, none can be greater than the need to advance the Kingdom and preach Jesus to all the nations!

ever lived. If being poor is synonymous with going to heaven or increases the chances of getting there, God would have made Solomon a very poor king indeed. However, King Solomon's untold riches and wealth given to him by God seems to fly in the face of such foolish thinking.

SOLOMON'S
MILITARY AND ECONOMIC POWER

So Solomon came to Jerusalem from the high place that was at Gibeon, from before the tabernacle of meeting, and reigned over Israel. And Solomon gathered chariots and horsemen; he had one thousand four hundred chariots and twelve thousand horsemen, whom he stationed in the chariot cities and with the king in Jerusalem. Also the king made silver and gold as common in Jerusalem as stones, and he made cedars as abundant as the sycamores, which are in the lowland.
2 Chronicles 1:11-15

King Solomon's military and economic power was unmatched in ancient history. The Bible tells us that King Solomon had fourteen hundred chariots. This is a lot of chariots. It's the equivalent of owning fourteen hundred military grade Humvees to carry troops to war. Additionally, Solomon had twelve thousand horsemen, which means that he owned more than twelve thousand horses for military purposes only. No matter how you slice this pie King Solomon had to be very rich to sustain such a large military force. You cannot take care of over twelve thousand horses and horsemen on a poor man's budget.

"Also the king made silver and gold as common in Jerusalem as stones, and he made cedars as abundant as the sycamores, which are in the lowland..." (2 Chronicles 1:15). This last part of the biblical text is quite mind-boggling to me. How rich do you have to

be to make gold and silver as common as stones on the ground? If this passage was not in the Bible I would never have believed it. Currently gold is trading just over $1320 per ounce of 99.9% grade of gold on the Stock Market. Can you imagine how rich the United States of America would be if 99.9% pure grade-gold became as common to all US citizens as the stones on the ground? Some of the poorest Israelites under King Solomon's reign would be considered millionaires in today's economy. If you had any doubt as to whether or not God wants His children wealthy you have only to look at King Solomon and doubt no more!

OBEDIENCE & SERVING
GOD = PROSPERITY

If they obey and serve Him, they shall spend their days in prosperity, And their years in pleasures. Job 36:11

The deeper we study the Scriptures the more it becomes obvious that the Constitution of the Kingdom includes a subsection that addresses our "covenant of prosperity." Job was one of the richest and godliest men in the land of Uz so it's befitting that it is in the book of Job where we find a powerful scripture on the covenant of prosperity. I want us to examine this scripture with forensic aptitude.

It starts with a very interesting conditional tenet which is the trigger to the entire covenant of prosperity; *"If they obey and serve*

Him." This conditional tenet makes obedience and serving God precursors to true Kingdom prosperity. In other words, wealth and riches obtained by circumventing heartfelt service and obedience to God will not benefit anyone in the light of eternity. Most of the wealth and riches obtained by Kingdom entrepreneurs that circumvent obedience and service to God do not last long. Most importantly such wealth will never bring peace of mind.

Nevertheless, what is abundantly clear is that God's Word promises that if we obey and serve Him, *"we shall spend our days in prosperity, and our years in pleasures!"* The word "spend" in the text is a marketplace term. The word "spend" typically implies the use of currency or capital towards the purchase of something we want or desire. God promises that if we obey and serve Him, He will give us more than enough cash (resources) "to spend the rest of our days on earth in peace and prosperity." The last part of the verse is even more interesting as it declares, "their years in pleasures!" This last part of the verse shows us what true prosperity buys; the ability to go beyond having our needs met to having our wants or luxuries fulfilled. Unfortunately, the religious spirits that control most followers of Christ will actively condemn members of the Body of Christ who are experiencing the aforementioned prosperous lifestyle. It amazes me just how many Christians are more tolerant of poverty than they are of prosperity. Surprisingly the same people will work 8-12 hour shifts to earn money to pay their monthly bills, but are put off by other Christians who are super-rich! It's the greatest of all paradoxes.

JOB: THE RICHEST MAN OF HIS TIME

There once was a man named Job who lived in the land of Uz. He was blameless—a man of complete integrity. He feared God and stayed away from evil. He had seven sons and three daughters. He owned 7,000 sheep, 3,000 camels, 500 teams of oxen, and 500 female donkeys. He also had many servants. He was, in fact, the richest person in that entire area. Job 1:1-3 NLT

The Bible gives Job a spectacular introduction. It first tells us his name and the land he lived in, Uz. Secondly, we are told that Job was *"blameless—a man of complete integrity. He feared God and stayed away from evil."* It's quite clear that the previous statement establishes Job's godly character. Job was not a godless or secular businessman by any means. The expression "he feared God" implies that Job had a very real and meaningful relationship with God. In this reference, the word fear is more accurately interpreted "reverence" meaning deep respect. In other words, Job reverenced God; it is difficult to have reverence or deep respect for someone unless you know them intimately. The expression "stayed away from evil" implies that Job had a very good and clear sense of right from wrong. He was a man of clear moral clarity.

Finally, the expression, *"He owned 7,000 sheep, 3,000 camels, 500 teams of oxen, and 500 female donkeys. He also had many servants. He was, in fact, the richest person in that entire area;"* introduces us to Job's financial status which flies in the face

43

of those who think that godliness cannot be congruent with wealth. The Bible goes out of its way to record and inform us of Job's net worth. If Job's social and economic status were not an integral part of Job's story, the Holy Spirit would have excluded them from the holy writ. The Bible doesn't just say that Job was rich; it makes sure we are aware that he was the richest man of his day! I hope and pray that Job's story is deepening your belief that God does want His people to be wealthy, in finances, not just righteousness!

IS GOD RICH?

The twelve gates were twelve pearls: each individual gate was of one pearl. And the street of the city was pure gold, like transparent glass. Revelation 21:21

We must now ask ourselves an equally important question. "Is God rich?" The question sounds quite simple but deeply profound and its ramifications far-reaching. The writer of the book of Revelation seems to think so. As the above scripture states *"and the street of the city was pure gold, like transparent glass."* Can you imagine any metropolitan city with streets paved with pure gold; gold so pure it looks like transparent glass? I must say this is majestic opulence beyond anything I have ever seen or heard of in this world. Any metropolitan city with streets paved in gold would be one of the richest cities in the entire world. There would be no poor person within the sphere of such a city. A city paved with gold; is this some childish fantasy? Not even close, because I am actually describing the present state of the New Jerusalem, the City of the Living God (Hebrews 12:24). Wow! God has an entire city with streets paved with pure gold. "Is God rich?" Yes, you better believe He is! God is more than super-rich; the richest persons on earth, including King Solomon are mere peasants compared to God's personal net worth.

Jesus told us in the disciples' prayer (commonly known as the Lord's prayer), that when we pray, we ought to begin by saying, *"Our Father who art in heaven, hallowed be your name, thy kingdom come, thy will be done here on earth as it is in heaven."* (Matthew 5:9-13). Notice that in this model prayer, Jesus says "thy will be done here on earth as it is in heaven" meaning that it is God's will for earth to reflect the atmosphere, culture, spirit, status and government of the Kingdom of Heaven. It stands to reason that if God lives in a city with streets paved with gold and it is His will that earth be a mirror image of heaven; then it's okay for us be rich here on earth. I rest my case.

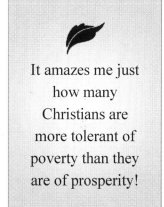

It amazes me just how many Christians are more tolerant of poverty than they are of prosperity!

GOD'S INCREASE PHILOSOPHY

Look to Abraham your father, and to Sarah who bore you;
For I called him alone, and blessed him and increased him.
Isaiah 51:2

The above scripture showcases a divine characteristic that is common to the person of God throughout Scripture, which is, God is a God of increase! In other words, God has a deep seated and divine "increase philosophy" in His very essence! In the above passage of Scripture God admonishes us to "look to Abraham and Sarah." God wants us to know that when He redeemed them (Abraham and Sarah), they did not have much to speak of in terms of material wealth. Abraham and Sarah were also poor in terms of human resources. They had no child of their own until God blessed them with a child (Isaac) who became a "multitude of tribes." God is essentially telling us that He was the One who was behind Abraham's blessings, wealth and increase. The Apostle Paul informs us that we can surely plant the seed and water it but only the Lord can cause the seed to

We must now ask ourselves an equally important question. "If God is rich, can His people be rich?"

increase (1 Corinthians 3:6 KJV). This means that increase is inherently supernatural! *Thus says the Lord, your Redeemer, the Holy One of Israel: "I am the Lord your God, who teaches you to profit, who leads you by the way you should go."* (Isaiah 48:17).

If you ever doubted that God has a serious increase philosophy in His dealings with mankind you need look no further than Isaiah 48:17. Listen to this, *"Thus says the Lord, your Redeemer, the Holy One of Israel: I am the Lord your God, who teaches you to profit, who leads you by the way you should go."* This passage of Scripture also explains why most Jewish people have no problem with becoming super-rich wherever they are domiciled in the world. How can you honestly explain the fact that Jews make up about 2% of the world's population and yet control a large percentage of the world's total wealth? Maybe it's because they grew up listening to their parents and Rabbis quote Isaiah 48:17 in their hearing. Since faith comes by hearing the Word of God most Jewish people may have an inbuilt belief that God wants them to be wealthy. This is not often the case with Christ's Gentile bride. Hopefully anointed books such as this one will help begin to turn the tide towards a radical increase philosophy in the Gentile Church.

"I am the Lord your God, who teaches you to profit, who leads you by the way you should go." I was immediately captivated by the expression, "I am the Lord your God, who teaches you to profit." Wow, what a Scripture! Do you mean to tell me that God wants to actively teach His children how to achieve profit in every venture that they are involved in, business or otherwise? What is of note here is the usage of the word profit in the ancient text. Profit is not a religious term; it's a business term. The essence of doing business or entrepreneurship is to produce a profit! Profit is what is left over in a profit and loss statement after operating expenses have been subtracted from earnings. God is essentially saying that He is the God who teaches us (His children) how to have a profitable business.

"Who leads you by the way you should go," is the final expression of the passage and means that God will lead the way in taking us to areas that will prove profitable for us. This is why we cannot lean on our own understanding but we must acknowledge the Lord in all our ways and He will direct our paths. (Proverbs 3:5-6) I want every person or Kingdom entrepreneur reading this book to understand that the Holy Spirit longs to lead you into areas of profit! This means that incurring losses in business ventures may be the direct result of not listening to the Holy Spirit! The Holy Spirit is the Spirit that teaches all of us to make a profit!

Then he who had received the one talent came and said, 'Lord, I knew you to be a hard man, reaping where you have not sown, and gathering where you have not scattered seed. And I was afraid, and went and hid your talent in the ground. Look, there you have what is yours.' But his lord answered and said to him, 'You wicked and lazy servant, you knew that I reap where I have not sown, and gather where I have not scattered seed. So you ought to have deposited my money with the bankers, and at my coming I would have received back my own with interest. Therefore, take the talent from him, and give it to him who has ten talents. Matthew 25:24-28

When Jesus gave us the parable of the talent, He forever cemented the fact that God is serious about increase. In this parable, there were three servants who were given stewardship or responsibility over their master's resources. The first servant was given five talents, the second one two talents and the last one got one talent. After a while the master returned to see what His servants had done with the talents he had entrusted them with (a prophetic picture of the second coming of Christ). The first servant had turned his five talents into ten by righteous trading. In the same manner, the second servant had turned his two talents into five. But when the last servant came before his master, his story was a sad one to say the least. Essentially, he had made no profit with the one talent he had been given. To make matters worse the ungrateful and "unprofitable servant" accused His master of being a "ruthless Lord, who reaped where he did not sow!" His master was furious with him.

Here is what his master told him, *"You wicked and lazy servant, you knew that I reap where I have not sown, and gather where I have not scattered seed. So you ought to have deposited my money with the bankers, and at my coming I would have received back my own with interest."* It's worth noting here that the master gave his lazy and unprofitable servant, a marketplace strategy for acquiring minimal profit by simply depositing money in a bank savings account. In righteous judgment, the master took the one talent that he had given the unprofitable servant and gave it to the first servant who had earned him the most profit! Wow! Are you getting the picture?

JOSEPH OF ARIMATHEA WAS A RICH MAN

Now when evening had come, there came a rich man from Arimathea, named Joseph, who himself had also become a disciple of Jesus. This man went to Pilate and asked for the body of Jesus. Then Pilate commanded the body to be given to him. Matthew 27:57-58

There is absolutely no mistake with how the Holy Spirit sequences things in the Holy Scriptures. For instance, when the Bible introduces us to Job (Job 1:1-6), his name is mentioned first, then the land he lived in is mentioned second, his righteous and godly character is mentioned third and then his vast wealth was mentioned last.

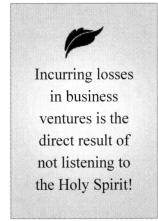

Incurring losses in business ventures is the direct result of not listening to the Holy Spirit!

This sequencing was a deliberate effort by the Holy Spirit to focus us on the essence of Job's story. This is because the entire emphasis of the book of Job is about the man, and how his godly character, devotion to God, stood the test of time against tremendous suffering.

On the other hand, when the Holy Spirit introduces us to Joseph of Arimathea, his wealth is mentioned first, then the city he lived in was mentioned second, and his name is mentioned third. This sequence is also divinely inspired and not happenstance. The reason the Bible introduces Joseph of Arimathea first as a "rich man" is because he was truly a very rich man and it was his wealth that qualified him to do the task the Lord was requiring of him. His vast wealth and political connections were the reason he was most qualified to rescue the lifeless body of Jesus on the cross. Said in another way, a poor man would never have fulfilled the demands of such a high level and sensitive Kingdom assignment! We will focus on this aspect of the "Joseph of Arimathea Calling" when we get to Chapter Five.

THE KINGDOM CONCEPT OF COMMONWEALTH

Now if God so clothes the grass of the field, which today is, and tomorrow is thrown into the oven, will He not much more clothe you, O you of little faith? "Therefore do not worry, saying, 'What shall we eat?' or 'What shall we drink?' or 'What shall we wear?' For after all these things the Gentiles seek. For your heavenly Father knows that you need all these things. But seek first the kingdom of God and His righteousness, and all these things shall be added to you.
Matthew 6:30-33

The Kingdom concept of "commonwealth" is one of great importance. Commonwealth is a concept that applies only to kingdoms as it does not exist in a democracy or republic. Commonwealth means that, all the wealth in a kingdom is made common to all its citizens. In kingdoms, the wealth of a king is not measured by how well the king lives but how well his subjects live.

51

If the subjects in a kingdom are poor, the king is also poor. This is because in a kingdom, the wealth or true value of that kingdom is measured by how much of its resources (wealth) is made available to all its citizens in a common and uniform experience.

Understanding the kingdom concept of commonwealth, Jesus makes a very compelling argument when he states in Matthew 6 *"Now if God so clothes the grass of the field, which today is, and tomorrow is thrown into the oven, will He not much more clothe you, O you of little faith? Therefore do not worry, saying, 'What shall we eat?' or 'What shall we drink?' or 'What shall we wear?' For after all these things the Gentiles seek. For your heavenly Father knows that you need all these things. But seek first the kingdom of God and His righteousness, and all these things shall be added to you."* Jesus starts out by drawing our attention to a very interesting fact: He lets us know that the "grass of the field" is part of the Kingdom of God. If the grass of the field is part of the Kingdom, God is personally responsible for clothing and feeding the grass even though it has a very short life cycle.

However, there is more, "will He not much more clothe you, O you of little faith?" Jesus now diagnoses why so many of His people live outside of their God-given right to commonwealth: they have so "little faith!" This is essentially the sickness of much of the global Body of Christ, too little faith! Jesus then declares that being obsessed with thinking about, "What shall we eat or what shall we drink, or 'what shall we wear;" is the mindset of a Gentile or a heathen. Wow! It is no wonder so many followers of Christ struggle continuously. They have abandoned their God given privilege to access the commonwealth of the kingdom in exchange for the daily grind of struggling and worrying about things!

PRIESTHOOD OF
THE MARKETPLACE

The LORD had said to Abram, "Leave your native country, your relatives, and your father's family, and go to the land that I will show you. I will make you into a great nation. I will bless you and make you famous, and you will be a blessing to others. I will bless those who bless you and curse those who treat you with contempt. All the families on earth will be blessed through you." Genesis 12:1-3

W HEN ABRAM ANSWERED the call of God and left the land of his nativity for the promised land, he did not know that his choice to obey the voice of God had placed him on a collision course with one of the most powerful spiritual Orders in all of creation. I have served God long enough to know that when we obey God and make choices that set us on a course toward our God-given destiny God will supernaturally weave Himself into the matrix of our lives. Years after

55

Abraham arrived in the promise land, he had a supernatural encounter with the lofty priesthood of Melchizedek (Genesis 14). Melchizedek was a priest of God Most High, who proceeded to confer a priestly blessing upon Abraham's life. By definition his names, "MelchiZedek" and "MelchiSalem" are translated "King of Righteousness" and "King of Peace" respectively. MelchiZedek was and still is the head of the Priesthood of the Kingdom. It goes without saying that it's impossible to be transformed into a bona fide Kingdom entrepreneur without understanding the gospel of the Kingdom.

DEFINING THE KINGDOM

But if I am casting out demons by the Spirit of God, then the Kingdom of God has arrived among you. Matthew 12:28

In our endeavor to transform the kingdoms (systems) of this world (Revelation 11:15) into the Kingdoms of God and of His Christ, we must first have a clear-cut definition of the term "Kingdom." Dr. Myles Munroe in his bestselling book <u>Rediscovering the Kingdom</u> gives us a definitive meaning for this very powerful word: "A kingdom is…The governing influence of a king over his territory, impacting it with his personal will, purpose, and intent, producing a culture, values, morals, and lifestyle that reflect the king's desires and nature for his citizens."[2]

From this definition, we can quickly see what God wants to do with the seven mountain-kingdoms on which the great whore, "Babylon the Great," sits (Revelation 17:1-9). God wants His covenant people, especially Kingdom entrepreneurs, to take the governing influence of His Kingdom and superimpose it over the spiritual and natural activities of the Seven Mountains of Culture. God desires to superimpose His personal will, purpose, and intent, upon the Mountains of Finance, Business, Law & Government, Media, Arts & Entertainment, Education, Family, and Religion/Church. God also wants the vehicle of human government to line up with His Kingdom agenda. The wealthy in the Kingdom of God are supposed to use their resources to help advance the Gospel of the Kingdom, instead of competing to acquire more wealth. This then begs the question, "Is there a priesthood of the Kingdom of God that Kingdom entrepreneurs can access to help them advance the kingdom in the marketplace?" The answer is a resounding "Yes!"

THE ORDER OF MELCHIZEDEK

The Lord said to my Lord, "Sit at My right hand, till I make Your Enemies Your footstool." ... The Lord has sworn and will not relent, "You are a priest forever according to the order of Melchizedek." Psalm 110:1,4

In Genesis 14:18-20 we learn: *"Then Melchizedek, King of Salem, brought out bread and wine; he was the priest of God Most High. And he blessed him and said: "Blessed be Abram of God Most*

High, Possessor of heaven and earth; And blessed be God Most High, who has delivered your enemies into your hand." And he gave him a tithe of all." Then in Hebrews 7:1-3 we learn more about this mysterious person: *For this Melchizedek, king of Salem, priest of the Most High God, who met Abraham returning from the slaughter of the kings and blessed him, to whom also Abraham gave a tenth part of all, first being translated "king of righteousness," and then also king of Salem, meaning "king of peace," without father, without mother, without genealogy, having neither beginning of days nor end of life, but made like the Son of God, remains a priest continually.*

One of the questions I get asked most often is, "What is the Order of Melchizedek?" Even though there are several scriptures (Psalm 110:1-5, Hebrews 5:1-10, 6:20, 7:1-14) in the Bible that directly tie the Lord Jesus Christ to the Order of Melchizedek many members of the Body of Christ are in a critical state of ignorance concerning the nature, scope and inner workings of this eternal royal priesthood. However, we all know that "ignorance is not bliss" especially on a subject so critical and central to advancing the Kingdom of God here on earth.

Since this question has popped up so many times, I have crystalized my answers to the question "What is the Order of Melchizedek?" below:

1. The Order of Melchizedek is the eternal royal priesthood of the eternal lamb (Jesus), (Revelation 5:4-6) which traces right

back to the Garden of Eden; when Adam and Eve first sinned and God slew an animal (shed blood) to atone for their sin. (Genesis 3:21)

2. The Order of Melchizedek is the eternal royal priesthood of Christ before He entered our planet through the virgin birth. (Psalm 110:1-4)

3. The Order of Melchizedek is the royal priesthood of the royal family of God in both heaven and earth. (1 Peter 2:9)

4. The Order of Melchizedek is the priesthood of the Kingdom that governs the activities of Kingdom citizens in the ministry, municipality and marketplace. (Genesis 14:18-20)

5. The Order of Melchizedek is the eternal order of a King of righteousness and King of peace. (Hebrews 7:1-3)

6. The Order of Melchizedek is the eternal priesthood of God that brought Abraham into a living covenant with God by initiating him into the priesthood of God through the sacrament of Holy Communion. (Genesis 14:18-20)

I hope that the above bullet points help clarify and crystalize your understanding of this powerful and eternal priesthood of the Lord Jesus Christ. For more information on the Order of Melchizedek, its scope, inner workings, and present day implications, I encourage you to read my book, The Order of Melchizedek. Below, I am going to share several defining aspects of the Order of Melchizedek that are worth repeating here because they give us a deeper understanding of this important priesthood of the marketplace for all Kingdom citizens.

IT IS A MARKETPLACE
AND PRIESTLY MINISTRY

The most unique aspect of the Order of Melchizedek is that, unlike the Levitical or Aaronic Priestly Order, this eternal Priestly Order is both a marketplace and priestly ministry. The High Priest of this eternal priestly Order is first and foremost a King who does priestly work. As a King, His influence extends well beyond the boundaries of the temple, right into the marketplace and the municipality. All kings own everything that is within their kingdom. As a King-Priest, Jesus

The wealthy in the Kingdom of God are supposed to use their resources to help advance the Gospel of the Kingdom.

Christ has ongoing dual influence over both the services of His priests in the temple and the activities of His people in the marketplace and municipality.

In contrast, the high priest under the Levitical priesthood and his staff of priests were not permitted to engage in any form of secular business activity outside the normal activities of servicing the spiritual needs of the people of Israel. The only time that the Levites sought secular employment was when the other eleven tribes neglected them. Moses made it very clear that God did not want the Levites to be involved in any form of secular business activity. He wanted them to focus their energy on servicing the spiritual needs of the people of Israel and those of the temple of God. To ensure that this was the case, God gave the tithes of the remaining eleven tribes of Israel to the tribe of Levi as an everlasting inheritance.

> *As for the tribe of Levi, your relatives, I will compensate them for their service in the Tabernacle. Instead of an allotment of land, I will give them the tithes from the entire land of Israel.* Numbers 18:21

ABRAM'S GREATEST EMBARRASSMENT

So Abram left Egypt and traveled north into the Negev, along with his wife and Lot and all that they owned. (Abram was very rich in livestock, silver, and gold). Genesis 13:1-2

While writing The Order of Melchizedek, the Holy Spirit gave me a revelation that shook me at the core of my being. This is what the Holy Spirit told me, "Son, as long as the Church thinks that Genesis 13:1-2 is an example of supernatural prosperity, it is never going to experience real Kingdom wealth." This statement shook me because I have used Genesis 13:1-2 many times in my teachings on Kingdom prosperity. The Holy Spirit continued, "Son, Genesis 13:1-2 is not the basis for real Kingdom wealth because Genesis 13:1-2 describes Abram's tainted wealth that he obtained by selling his wife to a demonic system." The Holy Spirit told me that tainted wealth can never form the basis of real Kingdom wealth. The Holy Spirit then said something to me that put the icing on the cake, "Many preachers and businessmen in the Body of Christ are doing the same thing that Abram did to his wife while he was in Egypt. They are prostituting the body (bride) of Christ or their business for money and then calling their resulting prosperity real Kingdom wealth." When the Holy Spirit said this to me I had to repent, because I discovered that I was also found wanting.

Abram replied to the king of Sodom, "I solemnly swear to the LORD, God Most High, Creator of heaven and earth, that I will not take so much as a single thread or sandal thong from what belongs to you. Otherwise you might say, 'I am the one who made Abram rich.'" Genesis 14:22-23

After Abram and Sarai left Egypt with an abundance of material possessions that Abram had obtained by deceiving the king of Egypt, the king told everyone who had an ear that he was the one who had made Abram rich. These malicious rumors followed Abram wherever he went. It was quite embarrassing to say the least. When Abram met Melchizedek (the priest of God Most High) he received a revelation on how he could sanctify his tainted wealth. Abram gave Melchizedek a tithe of all he had. This divinely inspired tithe not only destroyed the spirit of greed in Abram's life, it also became the supernatural purifying element, which sanctified everything that

Abram owned! Abram's tithes into this eternal king-priest brought everything that he owned into divine alignment. Abram's tithes into the Order of Melchizedek rolled away the reproach of Egypt from his life. This is why it is so important for the global Church to rediscover the Abrahamic tithing model.

When the king of Sodom offered Abram gold and silver from the treasuries of Sodom, Abram knew that he could not afford to make the same mistake twice. Abraham knew that if he took the money, the king of Sodom was going to join the king of Egypt in declaring that he was the one who had made Abram rich. Abram's refusal of the king of Sodom's generous offer underscores the power of tithing into the Order of Melchizedek. The Holy Spirit then concluded by telling me that real Kingdom wealth in Abram's life started right after His encounter with Melchizedek, the divine king-priest in Genesis 14. Melchizedek, the king-priest, brought Abraham into a living covenant with God. It follows then that the global church will never experience real Kingdom wealth until it understands what Christ has made available for it through His Order of Melchizedek priesthood.

THE KING OF SODOM

After Abram returned from his victory over Kedorlaomer and all his allies, the king of Sodom went out to meet him in the valley of Shaveh (that is, the King's Valley). Genesis 14:17

And with many other words he testified and exhorted them, saying, "Be saved from this perverse generation." Acts 2:40 NKJV

We will now examine how the Order of Melchizedek is designed to deliver Kingdom entrepreneurs from being corrupted by the demonic sodomic system, which is the principle of perversity that is inherent in all man-made institutions. I will show you how the Order of Melchizedek (the royal priesthood of Jesus) is designed to preserve Kingdom citizens who have vocations in a marketplace environment, which is controlled by systemic corruption and secularism. If you are a Kingdom businessman or

Moses made it very clear that God did not want the Levites to be involved in any form of secular business activity

woman I encourage you to prayerfully read this chapter. Please remember that Sodom was the most morally bankrupt nation among the countries of the East during Abraham's era. The people of Sodom and Gomorrah made the Egyptians look like saints.

The people of Sodom were ultra-social liberals who did not believe in heeding to any kind of divine restraint. Some of today's churches have been overtaken by the doctrine of demons which come in the form of a message of "greasy grace" that refuses to condemn sin in the church for fear of losing people who have not yet made up their minds to become disciples of Christ. Both Joseph's in the Bible were very rich men but they were still devout followers of God and in the case of Joseph of Arimathea, a disciple of Christ.

Let us take an introspective look at the king and people of Sodom to uncover what they represent, prophetically speaking. I will also show you how the Order of Melchizedek gives us the power to rise above the seductive influence of the demonic sodomic system. This is especially critical for those with vocations in the marketplace.

The following is a glossary of what the king of Sodom represents prophetically—a snapshot of the underlying essence of this demonic sodomic system.

1. The king of Sodom was the king of an ultra-liberal society in which every boundary of morality in the structure of the nation had been removed. This reminds me of the Sprite commercial which says "Obey your thirst!" In Sodom, everybody obeyed their thirst, whatever it was. This is the direction that the United States of America is sliding towards rapidly and the frontline of this culture war is the marketplace.

2. The king of Sodom was the king of a nation that celebrated every form of sexual perversion, including homosexuality and bestiality. Sexual perversity is quite prevalent in the marketplace today. They are many Kingdom businessmen and women, even pastors, who are struggling with an addiction to pornography. Unholy sexual affairs between CEOs and their secretaries are rampant in the marketplace,

even among the so-called "Christian businessmen." Most advertising campaigns for the selling of goods and services in the marketplace have strong sexual overtones.

3. The king of Sodom also represents the diabolical mismanagement of seed through inappropriate sexual intercourse between people of the same sex. This diabolical mismanagement of seed causes the seed of future apostles, prophets, pastors, presidents, and so forth to die before it could be birthed. This is not what God intended in the beginning when He created male and female as procreators of the second generation. This is the same spirit, which deceives many Kingdom businessmen and women, causing them to mismanage the financial resources (seeds) that are supposed to be used to advance the Kingdom. They end up purchasing multi-million-dollar luxury mansions in foreign lands that they only visit once a year. This diabolical mismanagement of Kingdom financial resources will come to an end, when Melchizedek's priesthood intercepts the power of the king of Sodom over His Kingdom citizens in the marketplace.

4. The king of Sodom completely destroyed the Mountain of Family within the structure of his nation. This would explain why Lot's daughters did not see anything wrong with having sex with their own father. (The mountain of family is what many call the institution of family.) Across the nations of the world there is a relentless attack on the institution of family in the marketplace. The primary victim of this relentless

demonic attack on the family is the traditional definition of marriage.

5. The king of Sodom also represents ill-gained financial resources, which were obtained by using demonic technology (corruption). The demonic sodomic system is behind the systemic corruption that is prevalent in many corporate boardrooms and corridors of government. Only those who are of the Order of Melchizedek can live above the reach of this demonic system. Kingdom businessmen and women must never allow themselves to participate in corrupt practices in order to secure a business contract. We must remember that we serve a God who can supply superabundantly in the worst economic conditions. If Kingdom business people engage in corruption they are opening the door for the devil to plunder their entire corporation.

6. The king of Sodom was a prophetic picture of the spirit of the anti-Christ. The spirit of the anti-Christ is the spirit that stands opposed to the advancement of the Kingdom of God and to anything that is Christ-like. Kingdom businessmen and women must never be ashamed of identifying themselves with the Kingdom of God in the marketplace. They must hold steadfast to both the values and the principles of the Kingdom and God will make sure that "all of these things" (profits) will be added to them.

7. The king of Sodom was so devoted to operating in spiritual darkness that the spirit of Satan manifested itself very

powerfully in his life. The demonic sodomic system is behind much of the satanism and infatuation with witchcraft that pervades most western nations. The king of Sodom (the devil) is behind the explosion of psychic phenomenon in the marketplace today. CEOs and some police departments are now consulting with psychics, when they should be consulting with God's prophets. Where are the "Josephs" and the "Daniels" who can bring the spirit of prophecy to the marketplace?

8. The king of Sodom is a prophetic representation of the spirit of Babylon, which is the principal spirit behind the systems of this world. The spirit of Babylon is an adulterous, covenant breaking spirit. This is the same spirit, which is behind much of the backstabbing and double dealing that is prevalent in corporate boardrooms and in the corridors of government. It is also the same spirit that causes many corporate women to sleep with their male counterparts to climb the corporate ladder. The Order of Melchizedek can save Kingdom citizens from being trapped in this perversity. The Order of Melchizedek will teach Kingdom businessmen and women how to honor all their verbal and contractual agreements with their vendors, creditors and business partners. You would be surprised just how untrustworthy many so called "Christian business men" really are!

As you may recall, in Chapter One I posed several questions that I will now answer:

- What priestly Order was Joseph operating under when he was in Egypt?
- Why did God give Joseph incredible favor with Pharaoh?
- What position did Joseph hold in Egypt?
- Why did God give Joseph such massive global influence?
- Why is God raising a "Corporate Joseph" in the earth today?

WHAT PRIESTLY ORDER WAS JOSEPH OPERATING UNDER WHEN HE WAS IN EGYPT?

Given the understanding of the Order of Melchizedek and it's king-priest mandate, it is safe to say that Joseph was operating under the Order of Melchizedek priesthood when he was stationed in Egypt. This is why Joseph could flow seamlessly in the priestly and marketplace (kingly) anointing. Joseph was as comfortable interpreting a prophetic dream as he was at interpreting a business plan (See Genesis 41:25-33.) Pharaoh saw this uncanny ability in Joseph and quickly promoted him.

The Bible also tells us that God testified that He knew that Abraham would command his sons to walk in the revelation that God

The Order of Melchizedek gives us the power to rise above the seductive influence of the demonic sodomic system.

had given him during his spiritual excursion. (see Genesis 18:17-19.) Joseph knew that he was operating under the highest priestly order in the entire universe. He was not intimidated to stand in front of Pharaoh, who was treated like a god in Egypt. Marketplace ministers who believe they are called to be "Josephs" to this generation would be well-advised to understand the Order of Melchizedek if they desire to become like the Joseph of old. Many Christian businessmen and women are quickly intimidated when they stand in front of renowned movers and shakers of this fallen world! Therefore, they become easy prey for the king of Sodom (the devil).

WHY DID GOD GIVE JOSEPH INCREDIBLE FAVOR WITH PHARAOH?

This second question underscores the most misunderstood aspect of Joseph's life. This misunderstanding has produced spiritual casualties among many so-called Christian or Kingdom businessmen and women. There are preachers who teach that God gave Joseph favor with Pharaoh so that Joseph could profit from the economy of Egypt. They conclude that without the favor that God gave him with Pharaoh, Joseph would never have become a powerful and rich man in Egypt. Regrettably, whenever our hearts have not yet been delivered from greed every revelation that God gives to us is quickly reduced to dollars and cents. Thus, the concept of Joseph having favor with Pharaoh for the purpose of exacting profit appeals to many of the so-called Christian businessmen and women.

Armed with this distorted view of Joseph, many marketplace ministers enter the marketplace with a driving passion to discover their "Pharaoh" and obtain their perceived "share of favor" so that they can profit financially from such relationships. Once they become rich after profiting, and sometimes pocketing millions of dollars from their network of relationships in the marketplace, these so-called Christian business men and women quickly conclude that they are walking in the Joseph anointing. But spiritually they leave the marketplace pretty much unchanged.

Turning Joseph into a rich or powerful person in Egypt was the last thing that God had in mind. God never buys into our egotistical nature. God is a God of purpose and His purpose never bows down to service our ego or our greed. There was a much higher purpose for the favor that God gave Joseph in Pharaoh's eyes. The money and power that Joseph ended up with in Egypt was simply a by-product of fulfilling a much higher purpose. It behooves us to discern this higher purpose.

WHAT POSITION DID JOSEPH HOLD IN EGYPT?

To discern and understand this higher purpose that compelled God to place Joseph in one of the loftiest positions in Egypt, we must first answer the question, "What position did Joseph hold in Egypt?" The answer to this question lies at the heart of understanding who Joseph was before God. When many of those who call themselves "Josephs," including those who teach on the subject, are asked this question, they quickly refer to Genesis 41:40-41. This passage reads as follows:

> *Thou shalt be over my house, and according unto thy word shall all my people be ruled: only in the throne will I be greater than thou. And Pharaoh said unto Joseph, See, I have set thee over all the land of Egypt.* Genesis 41:40-41

"Joseph was the second most powerful person in Egypt," I have heard many say after I asked them the question. But was Joseph really the second in command in Egypt? It is not enough to know what position a person holds in the realms of men. To truly discern the spiritual stature that God has given a man or woman in the Kingdom, we need to hear what God says about them. Ultimately, who people are to God trumps whatever title or rank they hold in the natural. In the natural order of things, Joseph was second in command in the land of Egypt. Did Joseph believe that he was second in command in the land of Egypt, or did God show him his actual position in Egypt in light of who he was in the Kingdom? Like the old folks used to say, let the Holy Book speak for itself: *And God sent me before you to preserve you a posterity in the earth, and to save your lives by a great deliverance. So now it was not you that sent me hither, but God: and he hath made me a **father to Pharaoh**, and lord of all his house, and a ruler throughout all the land of Egypt* (Genesis 45:7-8).

When Joseph revealed himself to his brothers, he told them the position that God had given him in Egypt. When you discover what God told Joseph, you will instantly become overwhelmed by the awesome position that God gave him in Egypt. Joseph tells his brothers "God has made me a father to Pharaoh!" Wow! Are you catching this? Joseph was not second in command in Egypt; he was the most powerful man in all of Egypt— powerful enough to spiritually father Pharaoh, the ruler of Egypt, and subsequently, his entire senate!!

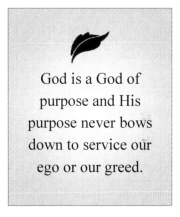

God is a God of purpose and His purpose never bows down to service our ego or our greed.

Suddenly everything becomes crystal clear. We have unmasked God's higher purpose for giving Joseph the favor that he had with Pharaoh. The favor was not given for the purpose of helping Joseph profit financially from the Egyptian economy. The supernatural favor was given to help him provide spiritual fathering into the life of Egypt's greatest orphan—Pharaoh himself! By fathering Pharaoh, Joseph was able to saturate the highest orders of government in Egypt with a fathering spirit from the Kingdom of God. Through this powerful fathering spirit, Joseph could effectively father every system of industry in the land of Egypt. Joseph established even the banking and real estate laws of Egypt. Instead of looking for favor for the sake of profit, real "Josephs" must look for divine opportunities to father many of the orphans who are in positions of great influence in the marketplace.

WHY DID GOD GIVE JOSEPH SUCH MASSIVE GLOBAL INFLUENCE?

Now therefore be not grieved, nor angry with yourselves, that ye sold me hither: for God did send me before you to preserve life. For these two years hath the famine been in the land: and yet there are five years, in the which there shall neither be earing nor harvest. And God sent me before you to preserve you a posterity in the earth, and to save your lives by a great deliverance. Genesis 45:5-7

We finally get to the point where we can now effectively answer the final piece of this puzzle. Why did God give Joseph such massive global influence? The answer is four-fold and deeply profound.

1. God gave Joseph massive global influence because he belonged to the highest spiritual order of priesthood any human being could ever belong to—the Order of Melchizedek. Since he belonged to the loftiest priestly order in all of creation, how could he ever be second in rank to a man (Pharaoh) who was under a demonic

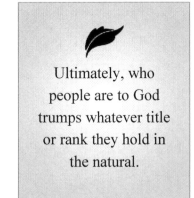

Ultimately, who people are to God trumps whatever title or rank they hold in the natural.

system? It is critical that the Body of Christ understand the Order of Melchizedek. When it does, the church will never ever accept second place to any demonic system, because it is of a higher order of priesthood.

2. God gave Joseph massive global influence because He could trust him with the level of favor that He had given him. God knew that Joseph was not going to allow his favor with the movers and shakers of Egypt to get to his heart or his head. I wonder how many Kingdom businessmen and women can pass this test.

3. God gave Joseph massive global influence because he knew that Joseph had been delivered from greed. God knew that Joseph was not going to allow his desire to profit financially from his high-profile connections to take priority over the need to father a generation of orphans in the marketplace. Even though God prospered Joseph financially, the money was simply a byproduct of his willingness to father Pharaoh and his senators. If present day "Josephs" can allow God to circumcise their hearts of the cancer of greed so they can become spiritual fathers to orphans in the marketplace, God will supernaturally give them more influence and money than they had ever imagined possible.

4. God gave Joseph massive global influence because God could trust him completely to use his lofty position to provide for the advancement of the Kingdom. God could trust him not to use his massive influence to exact personal vendettas. Joseph had the power to destroy his brothers who had sold him into slavery, but instead he chose to bless them because he recognized that they were fellow Kingdom citizens. Joseph told his brothers that God had raised him up to "preserve their lives" (Genesis 45:7). Joseph told his brothers that God had raised him up to preserve Abraham's inheritance in the nations of the earth.

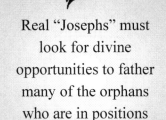

Real "Josephs" must look for divine opportunities to father many of the orphans who are in positions of great influence in the marketplace.

Today the church is being held hostage by millionaires and billionaires with an "orphan spirit" who claim to be "Josephs," but are not. True "Josephs" have no desire to use their financial power to manipulate God's leaders in the Kingdom. It is my prayer that all men and women who are truly called to be "Josephs" would be transformed by this revelation on the Order of Melchizedek.

WHY IS GOD RAISING A "CORPORATE JOSEPH" IN THE EARTH TODAY?

Finally, God is raising a "Corporate Joseph" in the earth today, because the spiritual and natural consequences of generations of greed-driven decisions are about to come to bear on the economies of many nations. The economies of most nations have been pillaged into bankruptcy by many power brokers in both the boardrooms of mega corporations and in the corridors of government. When the real estate bubble burst in the United States, it exposed just how deeply entrenched this culture of unrestrained greed really was. The sudden collapse of the American real estate market plunged the rest of the country into a deep and long recession. This created a famine in the land that had politicians pointing fingers at each other.

The interconnectedness of the global market to the US economy has sent spasms of financial and economic pain into every economy on earth. This has resulted in the famine caused by the greed of American politicians and businessmen to spread throughout the nations. Some nations are in complete and dire distress. The unemployment rate in Zimbabwe, for instance, stands at a whopping 90%! In the United States, the unemployment rate is rising steadily with no immediate end in sight to the worsening economic recession.

To deliver the Body of Christ from being destroyed by the consequences of the greed of worldly men and women, God has established a counter-strategy. God's counter-strategy to the growing pockets of famine in the nations of the world is to raise a "Corporate

77

Joseph" who will preserve the saints and sustain the ongoing work of advancing the Kingdom of God. But this "Corporate Joseph" will not rise in full stature until the global church begins to rediscover the Order of Melchizedek. The "Joseph of Arimathea Calling" requires that we understand and submit ourselves to the royal priesthood of Jesus Christ.

A BODY SHROUDED
IN HEATED CONTROVERSY

The ROOTS AND ORIGINS OF GOD'S purpose for creating the human race are found in the first two chapters of the book of Genesis. God wanted His spirit-children to become legal residents and guardians of the visible planet called Earth. This physical world that we live in was designed to be a spiritual colony of the Kingdom of heaven.

GOD'S ORIGINAL IDEA

Then God said, "Let us make human beings in our image, to be like us. They will reign over the fish in the sea, the birds in the sky, the livestock, all the wild animals on the earth, and the small animals that scurry along the ground." So God created human beings in his own image. In the image of God, he created them; male and female he created them. Then God blessed them and said, "Be fruitful and multiply. Fill the earth and govern it. Reign over the fish in the sea, the birds in the sky, and all the animals that scurry along the ground." Genesis 1:26-28

Genesis 1:26-28 uncovers God's plan and gives us insight into His original idea and intent for creating humankind. God never gives up on an original idea because God will not allow His Word to return to Him unfulfilled. God's Word will always prosper in the accomplishment of whatever God intended it to do. Please remember that God knows the end from the beginning; this is why there is no chance of failure for any of His original ideas.

So, what is God's original idea? To have spirit-children who can manage and govern the affairs of His invisible Kingdom here on earth.

THE MANIFEST SONS OF GOD

For the earnest expectation of the creation eagerly waits for the revealing of the sons of God. For the creation was subjected to futility, not willingly, but because of Him who subjected it in hope; because the creation itself also will be delivered from the bondage of corruption into the glorious liberty of the children of God. For we know that the whole creation groans and labors with birth pangs together until now. Romans 8:19-22 NKJV

When we fast-forward to the New Testament, we discover that God has not given up on His original idea. Even though the fall from grace of Adam and Eve created a short delay in the fulfillment of this divine mandate, God never ever gave up on the plan of having Spirit-led children who can forcefully advance and execute His Kingdom agenda here on earth.

What's more, Apostle Paul, in his epistle to the Romans, tells us that God went a step further and placed a deep groaning in all of creation for the manifestation of the true sons of God here on earth.

The apostle Paul tells us that all of creation will be delivered from the technology of sin and death through the ministry of the manifest sons of God. The ministry of the manifest sons of God will overturn the Adamic curse that was placed upon the whole of creation when Adam and Eve sinned and fell from dominion. What a powerful end-time ministry the sons of the Kingdom have been given!

God never ever gave up on the idea of having Spirit-led children on earth who can forcefully advance and execute His Kingdom agenda here on earth.

THE NEW CREATION

Therefore, from now on, we regard no one according to the flesh. Even though we have known Christ according to the flesh, yet now we know Him thus no longer. Therefore, if anyone is in Christ, he is a new creation; old things have passed away; behold, all things have become new. 2 Corinthians 5:16-17 NKJV

It is quite clear that Christ came to the earth for the primary purpose of restoring humankind to God's original idea for the human race. After the first Adam fell into sin and became a puppet of the devil, God had to find a way to legally restore the broken covenant of fellowship. Apostle Paul tells us that when any person is in Christ he or she becomes a new creation. When a person becomes a new creation, God cancels the power of past sins and iniquities from his or her life. The person truly becomes a brand-new person from the inside out. Said plainly, the "new creation" is the spiritual identity of the manifest sons of God for which all of creation is waiting.

JESUS WAS BORN; CHRIST WAS GIVEN

Without question, this is the great mystery of our faith: Christ was revealed in a human body and vindicated by the Spirit. He was seen by angels and announced to the nations. He was believed in throughout the world and taken to heaven in glory.
1 Timothy 3:16

One of the most important mysteries of God is the mystery of the incarnation. Apostle Paul tells us that the incarnation of Christ (God) into the human body is a "great mystery." Unfortunately, many ecclesiastical leaders and believers do not understand this great mystery. Many believers do not understand why the Word became flesh. After the fall of Adam and Eve in the Garden of Eden, humankind became shrouded completely in sin. The fall of Adam and Eve was so drastic that sin invaded every aspect of man's triune being. Man's spirit lost the life of God; his soul also became a prisoner of sin while death attached itself to man's physical body. Sin in the human nature spread like a malignant cancer to every fiber of man's being.

A total overhaul of man's entire nature was required. Humankind needed a brand-new spirit, soul, and body. What's more, sin had destroyed humankind's God-given capacity to become like God and represent Him fully. When Christ (the eternal Word and image of God) saw the utter depravity of humankind's condition, He knew that the only way humankind could ever become like God was if He became one of us. Thus, the Word became flesh through the virgin birth and God became one of us.

For a child is born to us, a son is given to us. The government will rest on his shoulders. And he will be called: Wonderful Counselor, Mighty God, Everlasting Father, Prince of Peace.
Isaiah 9:6

Therefore, from now on, we regard no one according to the flesh. Even though we have known Christ according to the flesh, yet now we know Him thus no longer. Therefore, if anyone is in Christ, he is a new creation; old things have passed away; behold, all things have become new. 2 Corinthians 5:16-17 NKJV

These Scriptures are probably two of the most misunderstood passages in the Bible. We can never appreciate who Christ and Jesus really are if we remain ignorant as to what truly transpired in both the incarnation and the resurrection. Additionally, if we don't understand the spiritual dynamics of the "Dichotomy of Christ" we will also fail to appreciate the priceless value of what Joseph of Arimathea did in rescuing the body of Jesus. I will spend some time uncovering these two great mysteries.

In Isaiah 9:6, the prophet Isaiah makes two very important prophetic statements that we need to understand if we want to know Christ the hope of glory. The prophet says, "for unto us a Child is born" and "unto us a Son is given." Herein lies the entire mystery of Christ's incarnation. The "Child" who was "born" is Jesus of Nazareth. The "Son" who was "given" to us is Christ (the eternal Word and express image of the invisible God.) (See John 1:1.)

Interestingly enough, the angel who appeared to Joseph in a dream made it quite clear that Jesus of Nazareth was the "Child" who was to be born; whereas the apostle John informs us that Christ was the Son of God who was given (gifted) to us. Take a look at these three Scriptures and see if they match up with what the prophet Isaiah told us in Isaiah 9:6:

As he considered this, an angel of the Lord appeared to him in a dream. "Joseph, son of David," the angel said, "do not be afraid to take Mary as your wife. For the child within her was conceived by the Holy Spirit. And she will have a son, and you are to name him Jesus, for he will save his people from their sins" Matthew 1:20-2

For God loved the world so much that he gave his one and only Son, so that everyone who believes in him will not perish but have eternal life. John 3:16

So the Word became human and made his home among us. He was full of unfailing love and faithfulness. And we have seen his glory, the glory of the Father's one and only Son. John 1:14

The Bible makes important distinctions between Christ's humanity and His divinity. The Jesus part of His title (name) deals solely with the trappings of His humanity; whereas the Christ part of His title (name) deals solely with His divinity. Jesus Christ saves us from sin through His humanity, but He glorifies us into Christ-like son-ship after we are born-again through His divinity. He redeems us from sin through His humanity, but He exalts us to reign with Him in righteousness through His divinity. His ministry to us in His humanity had limitations on it, but His ministry to us in His divinity will last throughout eternity. What is abundantly clear is that Christ would never have accomplished all He did if He did not possess a physical body of flesh. For one thing, there would never have been a crucifixion or resurrection if it were not for His physical body of flesh.

GOD'S PURPOSE FOR THE BODY

God never creates anything without having a purpose. God is a God of purpose. Purpose is the reason and motivation behind everything God has ever done. So here is the million-dollar question, "What is God's purpose for forming the body?" The following is a list of items that relate to God's purpose for the physical body.

God never ever gave up on the idea of having Spirit-led children on earth who can forcefully advance and execute His Kingdom agenda here on earth.

1. To house, man's spirit and soul during his earthly pilgrimage (Genesis 2:7, 1 Thessalonians 5:23).

2. To make man's spirit legal here on earth, because spirits without physical bodies are illegal here on earth (Matthew 12:43-45).

3. To serve as a temple of the Holy Spirit here on earth (1 Corinthians 6).

4. To serve as a vehicle for allowing man's spirit to do and manifest God's will here on earth as it is in heaven (Hebrews 10:4-5).

5. To house, man's spirit until the fulfillment of His God given destiny or assignment (2 Tim 4:7-10).

6. To serve as a vehicle of procreation for more physical bodies that God needs to house more human spirits on assignment from heaven. The Bible calls the act of procreation between

man and woman "child bearing or the fruit of the body" (Psalm 132:11).

7. To make up in our physical bodies what's lacking in the suffering of Christ. (Galatians 6:17) Sometimes our suffering for Christ and our ultimate triumph in our physical body can inspire faith and hope in God in those who are lost.

8. To carry out physical activity such as walking, running, working, eating, painting, fighting, hunting, driving or sex just to name a few. Without the aid of the physical body none of us can lift a finger to help anybody.

9. To assist man's spirit in generating spiritual power for God's work through the act of prayer and fasting. (Matthew 17:21)

10. To assist man's spirit in generating spiritual power and intimacy with God through the act of praise and worship. (Psalm 150, Exodus 12:27)

11. To assist humans in bearing each other's physical burdens here on earth. Have you ever tried to help anybody lift his or her heavy luggage when you are sick? Better still have you ever seen a dead uncle show up to help you carry heavy luggage to the car?

12. To assist man's spirit in carrying and demonstrating God's invisible government here on earth. (Isaiah 9:6-7)

I am reminded of a friend of mine who was the senior pastor of a thriving church in Chicago. He was an excellent governor and ran his church like a well-oiled machine. He died suddenly from cancer. After his death, the church split into several warring factions until they lost their beautiful 1500 seat congregation that he had built. I know that had he lived, he would have never allowed the infighting that took over his flock. Unfortunately, he lost his physical body to cancer, so his spirit became

Purpose is the reason and motivation behind everything God has ever done

illegal here on earth. He had to go to heaven. I wonder how he felt as he watched from the balconies of heaven the church he built disintegrate into various factions?

I hope and pray that reading through God's purpose for the physical body will inspire a radical change in the way you steward your physical body. The aforementioned purposes of God for forming the physical body underscore why the healing ministry is so important. The healing ministry is God's divine emergency system for reversing the destruction of the physical body by demonic powers. However, entering a healthy lifestyle is far more important than trying to secure healing each time we get sick. Most importantly, I hope you are coming to terms with the priceless importance of what Joseph of Arimathea did by rescuing and preserving the body of

Jesus. Without having His physical body, Christ would have been illegal here on Earth.

THE BODY OF JESUS

Therefore, when He came into the world, He said: "Sacrifice and offering You did not desire, But a body You have prepared for Me. In burnt offerings and sacrifices for sin, You had no pleasure. Then I said, 'Behold, I have come—In the volume of the book it is written of Me—To do Your will, O God.'" Hebrews 10:5-7

After the fall of man in the Garden of Eden, man's moral and spiritual decline was very rapid: by the time you get to Genesis Chapter 6 the earth was filled with violence. Sexual intercourse between the daughters of men and fallen angels was commonplace. God even repented for creating mankind. It would seem as though man's fate was forever sealed to a life imprisoned by sin and separated from God. In moments of divine inspiration some of the prophets of Israel prophesied about a future world Messiah who would restore the broken fellowship between man and God.

Most famous among these ancient prophecies is the cry of the Prophet Isaiah, *"therefore the Lord himself shall give you a sign; behold a virgin shall conceive, and bear a son, and shall call his name Immanuel."* (Isaiah 7:14). The name Immanuel carried the spiritual technology that God the Son would use to become legal here on earth. The name Immanuel literally means "God inside a human body." God supernaturally crafted Himself an incorruptible body inside Mary's (Miriam) womb. The writer of Hebrews (Hebrews 10:5) says it this way, "a body have you prepared me!" The writer of the book of Hebrews is reporting in the third person, which means that God opened his spiritual ears to hear a conversation between God the Father and God the Son from eternity past. However, the succeeding verse is equally important. Then said I, Lo, I come in the volume of the book (the Torah) it is written of me, to do thy will, O God.

After declaring "a body you have prepared for me;" God the Son (Christ) makes a very interesting statement that showcases the importance of a "prepared body" in doing of God's will here on earth. He declares, *"I come in the volume of the book (the Torah) it is written of me, to do thy will, O God."* (Hebrews 10:4-5). This statement seems to be suggesting that the reason the will of God is rarely done on earth is because the physical bodies of so many of God's people are not "prepared to be a living sacrifice unto God," (Romans 12:1) in total obedience 24/7. Here we clearly see that it's practically impossible to do the will of God here on earth without engaging man's physical body, making man's physical body just as important as his spirit in doing God's will. This would explain why the devil does not really care how willing our spirit is, if our physical body (flesh) is weak.

In the incorruptible physical body of Jesus Christ, God had finally found Himself a living sacrifice worthy of a "once and for all atonement." In His delight at the prepared body of Jesus, the Lord then drops a bombshell revelation: He declares that even though the entire Levitical priesthood was based on the daily sacrifices of animals to atone for the sins of the people, God was never ever satisfied by any of it. However, the value of the incorruptible and sinless body of Jesus was such that the offering of His physical body on the cross, would atone for the sins of all mankind, once and for all (Hebrews 10:10).

The healing ministry is God's divine emergency system for reversing the destruction of the physical body by demonic powers.

THE PRICELESSNESS
OF THE BODY OF JESUS

I have set the Lord always before me; because He is at my right hand I shall not be moved. Therefore, my heart is glad, and my glory rejoices; My flesh (body) also will rest in hope. For You will not leave my soul in Sheol, nor will You allow Your Holy One to see corruption. Psalm 16:8-10

The pricelessness of the body of Jesus can never be overestimated. The physical body of Jesus Christ is truly our life, as follows:

1. Without the sacrifice of the body of Jesus on the cross there would be no hope for the redemption of our physical bodies.
2. Without the sacrifice of the body of Jesus on the cross God would never have been able to judge sin in the body of Jesus.
3. Without the sacrifice of the body of Jesus on the cross all of us would be ruled by the fallen, evil dictates of our "old man" (unregenerate nature). Thankfully our old nature of sin was crucified on the cross in the body of Jesus.
4. Without the sacrifice of the body of Jesus on the cross there would be no resurrection of the dead. Resurrection of the dead requires the resurrection of the physical body into an immortal body.

THE CALL OF JOSEPH OF ARIMATHEA

Now when evening had come, there came a rich man from Arimathea, named Joseph, who himself had also become a disciple of Jesus. This man went to Pilate and asked for the body of Jesus. Then Pilate commanded the body to be given to him. Matthew 27:57-58

Each one of us is born by purpose, for a purpose. Among the over five billion humans who currently live on earth no one has the
92

exact same fingerprints. If this does not suggest divine intent, I don't know what will. During the days of the Lord's earthly pilgrimage there was a certain man by the name of Joseph of Arimathea. All the Bible tells us about this amazing man is found in three verses of Scripture. We will discuss the amazing call of Joseph of Arimathea in depth in the next chapter. But I will give you some quick highlights, as follows:

1. He was a rich man
2. He was a disciple of Jesus
3. He was very politically connected
4. He rescued the body of Jesus from the cross and gave it a prestigious burial among the tombs of the rich.

Joseph of Arimathea, a prominent council member, who was himself waiting for the Kingdom of God, coming and taking courage, went in to Pilate and asked for the body of Jesus. Mark 15:43

I believe Joseph of Arimathea's entire existence on earth was designed to put in him a place of prominence so he could negotiate with the Roman government for the right to bury the physical body of Jesus. There is no biblical evidence that Jesus and Joseph of Arimathea ever met in person. Notwithstanding, somehow, during the ministry of Jesus, Joseph of Arimathea became a believer in the promised Jewish Messiah. I believe the reason the Bible mentions the fact that he was rich is to imply that his wealth is what gave him an audience with Pontius Pilate.

I am confident that had he been a poor man, Pontius Pilate would never have given him the time of day. The Romans were a very proud people who looked down on those with no economic or social status. The fact that Joseph of Arimathea could secure an audience with the governor from Rome means that his wealth and social status were well known. In the previous section, we established just how valuable the body of Jesus was to God's plan of redemption; can you also see how valuable the call of Joseph of Arimathea was to God's Kingdom? Without Joseph of Arimathea, those opposed to Jesus' mission would have probably desecrated or cremated His body. Mary Magdalene and the disciples would have had no tomb to visit on that fateful resurrection morning. The Body of Christ is full of people like Joseph of Arimathea, whose primary call is to preserve the Body of Christ. Churches that do not believe in financial prosperity will crucify their Joseph of Arimathea's.

RESCUING THE LIFELESS BODY OF JESUS

Now when evening had come, there came a rich man from Arimathea, named Joseph, who himself had also become a disciple of Jesus. This man went to Pilate and asked for the body of Jesus. Then Pilate commanded the body to be given to him. When Joseph had taken the body, he wrapped it in a clean linen cloth, and laid it in his new tomb, which he had hewn out of the rock; and he rolled a large stone against the door of the tomb, and departed. Matthew 27:57-60

Let us ask ourselves the question, "What can be more important than rescuing the body of Jesus?" I find it difficult to even imagine anything that would surpass such a task in importance. Since the body of Jesus is more accurately the Body of Christ (for Christ is an uncreated Spirit and the second member of the Godhead) we can also rephrase this question as such, "What can be more important than rescuing the Body of Christ?" Since the resurrection and ascension of the Lord Jesus Christ, His universal body has increased tremendously. Instead of the body of Jesus, which was localized in one geographical location in one person, the Lord Jesus Christ, we have now migrated into the Body of Christ. The Body of Christ is Christ's universal body. The Body of Christ is His "church universal" united by the covenant bonds of His shed blood and finished work.

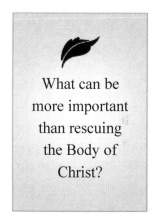

What can be more important than rescuing the Body of Christ?

The Body of Christ is what the Spirit calls the bride and the Lord Jesus is our bridegroom. Everything the Lord Jesus did on the cross was to give birth to His universal body, the church. It goes without saying that had Joseph of Arimathea not rescued the body of Jesus and prepped it for burial in keeping with what the prophets had prophesied, the resurrection story would have become more complicated. Imagine what would have happened had the Sanhedrin council got hold of the body of Jesus and chose to cremate it? While I am firm believer that "with God nothing is impossible," you have to admit that the resurrection story would have been that much more difficult to pull off. Not to mention that King David's prophecy *"for You will not leave my soul in Sheol, nor will You allow Your Holy One to see corruption"* (Psalm 16) would have remained unfulfilled.

The last part of this messianic prophecy, *"nor will You allow Your Holy One to see corruption,"* which is found in Psalm 16:10, is a direct reference to the fact God would not allow the body of Jesus to suffer decomposition. The million-dollar question is "How did God fulfill this part of the ancient prophecy?" The answer stares us in the face; it was through the ministry of a rich man, by the name of Joseph of Arimathea. During the time the Lord Jesus was on earth, only the wealthy had access to special and costly embalming oils. Some of these oils were imported directly from the best Egyptian embalmers. These oils slowed down the decomposition of a dead body. Joseph of Arimathea applied such oils to the body of Jesus as he prepped it for burial. It is quite clear to me that no one can fulfill the calling of Joseph of Arimathea, who has no passion to use his or her wealth to rescue the Body of Christ.

A BODY SHROUDED
IN HEATED CONTROVERSY

Now after the Sabbath, as the first day of the week began to dawn, Mary Magdalene and the other Mary came to see the tomb. And behold, there was a great earthquake; for an angel of the Lord descended from heaven, and came and rolled back the stone from the door, [a] and sat on it. His countenance was like lightning, and his clothing as white as snow. And the guards shook for fear of him, and became like dead men. But the angel answered and said to the women, "Do not be afraid, for I know that you seek Jesus who was crucified. He is not here; for He is risen, as He said." Matthew 28:1-6

The stolen body hypothesis posits that the body of Jesus Christ was stolen from his burial place. His tomb was found empty not because he was resurrected, but because the body had been hidden somewhere else by the apostles or unknown persons. Both the stolen body hypothesis and the debate over it presumes to refute the basic historicity of the gospel accounts of the tomb discovery. The stolen body hypothesis finds the idea that the body was not in the tomb plausible because it considers it more likely that early Christians had been misled into believing the resurrection by the theft of Jesus's body.

The hypothesis has existed since the days of early Christianity; it is discussed in the Gospel of Matthew, generally agreed to have been written between AD 70 and 100. Matthew's gospel raises the hypothesis only to refute it; according to Matthew's account, the claim the body was stolen is a lie spread by the Jewish high priests.

Now while they were going, behold, some of the guard came into the city and reported to the chief priests all the things that had happened. When they had assembled with the elders and consulted together, they gave a large sum of money to the soldiers, saying, "Tell them, 'His disciples came at night and stole Him away while we slept.' And if this comes to the governor's ears, we will appease him and make you secure." *So they took the money and did as they were instructed; and this saying is commonly reported among the Jews until this day.* Matthew 28:11-15

It is quite clear from reading the above passages of Scripture that there was great and heated controversy surrounding the body of Jesus. The speed with which the high priest and the Sanhedrin council created the "stolen body hypothesis" further demonstrates the vast importance of what Joseph of Arimathea did. Since he went through the official political channels to secure the body of Jesus from the cross there was a visible and legitimate paper trail of how he secured the body of Jesus, prepped it for burial and buried it in his tomb.

Since the enemies of Jesus, were afraid that Jesus' disciples might steal the body so they could claim He had been resurrected they petitioned Pilate to put a Roman security detail to guard the tomb of

Jesus. I am so glad that they did because their actions further authenticated Jesus's resurrection. Most Roman soldiers would rather die than fail to secure a tomb that they were instructed to secure at the decree of one of Caesar's governors. On resurrection morning, a violent earthquake shook the tomb and then a shining angel appeared. The angel rolled away the huge stone that was sealing the tomb. All the Roman soldiers saw this firsthand and fainted because of fear. After they recovered they ran to the high priest and Sanhedrin council to tell them the truth of what had just transpired. Petrified by the

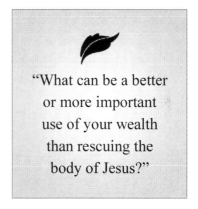

"What can be a better or more important use of your wealth than rescuing the body of Jesus?"

earth shattering implications of Jesus' resurrection, the high priest bribed the Roman soldiers to change their story. The soldiers were instructed to say that Jesus' disciples had stolen His body. How ironic that a few unarmed fishermen would overpower a heavily armed Roman security detail just to steal a dead body! It is quite ridiculous to say the least.

JOSEPH OF ARIMATHEA

ACCORDING to Britannia, Joseph of Arimathea was a wealthy disciple of Jesus. In Matthew's account (27:57-60) he asked Pontius Pilate for permission to take Jesus' body and prepare it for burial. He used his own tomb to bury Jesus. Legend has it that Joseph acquired his wealth in the metals trade, some of it with Britain. According to legend he accompanied Apostle Philip, Lazarus and Mary Magdalene on a preaching mission trip to Gaul (France). He brought with him two cruets, one containing the blood and the other, the sweat of Christ. These items are known as The Holy Grail, and were the object(s) of the quests of the Knights of King Arthur's Round Table. One legend goes on to suggest that Joseph hid the Grail in Chalice Well at Glastonbury for safe-keeping. Joseph of Arimathea is venerated as a saint by the Roman Catholic, Eastern Orthodox, and some Protestant churches. The traditional Roman calendar marked his feast day on March 17, but he is now listed, along with Saint Nicodemus, on August 31 in the Martyrologium Romanum. Eastern Orthodox chur ches commemorate him on the Third Sunday of Pascha (i.e., the second Sunday after Easter)[3]. While it is certainly not my intention to dwell on the history of Joseph of Arimathea, his background provides some context as to his prominence in society and how he obtained an audience with Pontius Pilate.

History is what we are left with when men are dead. On the other hand, divinely inspired revelation is what gives both context and meaning to the lives of these great heroes of faith. Revelation gives us a fresh, God-inspired perspective on the lives of these great heroes of faith and the principles of the Kingdom that they embraced that make them worth emulating. In this chapter, I will focus my attention on giving you the revelation the Holy Spirit gave me, concerning Joseph of Arimathea. I especially dedicate this chapter to the very wealthy in the Body of Christ who have not yet discovered the true purpose of their wealth! I also dedicate this chapter to the hundreds of Kingdom businessmen and women who are looking for scriptural and pragmatic solutions for navigating political landmines in their endeavor to grow their businesses in today's ever evolving marketplace.

Now when evening had come, there came a rich man from Arimathea, named Joseph, who himself had also become a disciple of Jesus. This man went to Pilate and asked for the body of Jesus. Then Pilate commanded the body to be given to him. When Joseph had taken the body, he wrapped it in a clean linen cloth, and laid it in his new tomb, which he had hewn out of the rock; and he rolled a large stone against the door of the tomb, and departed. Matthew 27:57-60

The above passage of scripture introduces us to the amazing story of a man who seemingly comes from nowhere, Joseph of Arimathea: however, the principles, patterns, characteristics and Kingdom concepts contained in his story are both precious and timeless. The story of Joseph of Arimathea contains the nomenclature of a true Kingdom entrepreneur and the true purpose of wealth. The late Dr. Myles Munroe has said, "Where purpose is not known abuse is truly inevitable." Many wealthy people in the world and even in the Body of Christ do not understand the true purpose of wealth. Consequently, they misdirect their wealth and forfeit their true potential in Christ. It's been my humble observation that the most dangerous tool a human can have is wealth without a purpose. We will now begin to mine the story of Joseph of Arimathea for all the precious nuggets that it contains for today's Kingdom businessmen and women. I must first point out that there are fourteen unique features of the "Joseph of Arimathea Calling" that every Kingdom entrepreneur ought to aspire to attain. The Lord showed me that these unique features augment the kind of Kingdom entrepreneur God wants to produce under the Order of Melchizedek (Hebrews 6:20). We will examine each of these unique features separately.

#1 - THERE CAME A RICH MAN

Now when evening had come, **there came a rich man** *from Arimathea, named Joseph, who himself had also become a disciple of Jesus.* Matthew 27:57

The first characteristic to note about Joseph of Arimathea is crystalized in the statement, "there came a rich man." This is perhaps one of the most important features of the Joseph of Arimathea calling. You can never fulfill the calling of Joseph of Arimathea if you are not rich. As noted previously, the sequencing the Bible uses when it

History is what we are left with when men are dead!

introduces a significant biblical character is quite important and is not subject to happenstance. In Joseph of Arimathea's case, the Bible focuses first and foremost on his economic and social status. It tells us…. "Now when evening had come, there came a **rich** man."

The Holy Spirit wants us to understand that Joseph of Arimathea's social and economic status, as a rich man is the primary reason the Lord chose him for such a historic and eternally important mission. In other words, this particular Kingdom assignment was beyond the reach of a poor man. There are some highly specialized Kingdom assignments that only rich or super-rich Kingdom citizens can be called upon to perform. For instance, if God wants a certain piece of prime real estate to be purchased for the purpose of advancing His Kingdom; He won't call upon one of his poor children to do it. He or she would have no cash flow to perform such a task. In another instance, if God wanted to demonstrate the superiority of His manifold wisdom among today's super-wealthy He would hardly use one of His poor children because the Bible says that the *"poor man's wisdom is despised"* (Ecclesiastes 9:16)! I have no intention to come across as elitist but to simply declare a plain biblical truth.

It is clear from the biblical text that it was Joseph of Arimathea's wealth that earned him an audience with Pontus Pilate, Governor of Rome, over the land of Palestine. One can deduct from the text that Joseph of Arimathea and Pontus Pilate already knew of each other. Given Joseph's social standing, they may have met each other at some high-level social or political gathering. The speed with which Pontus Pilate accommodated Joseph of Arimathea's visit suggests a prior relationship of some kind. You don't have to stretch your imagination to believe that a wealthy multi-millionaire might have a much easier time commanding an audience with the president of the United States. A poor man would have significant challenges trying to secure such an audience. Therefore, Kingdom entrepreneurs who have already achieved the status of being rich or super-wealthy must never be ashamed of their social and economic status in life. Church leaders must also stop using their skewed theology on prosperity to heap unnecessary religious guilt on rich or super-wealthy members of the Body of Christ.

#2 - FROM ARIMATHEA

*Now when evening had come, there came a rich man **from Arimathea**, named Joseph, who himself had also become a disciple of Jesus.* Matthew 27:57

The second feature about becoming a Joseph of Arimathea in the Kingdom is crystalized in the statement, "a rich man from Arimathea." According to Fosset's Bible Dictionary, Arimathea is also known as Ramathaim, the home of the prophet Samuel. In New Testament times it was situated NW of Jerusalem in the hill country of Ephraim. It is also where David came to Samuel (1 Samuel 19). The statement, "a rich man from Arimathea," tells a lot about Joseph of Arimathea. Firstly, it tells us that Joseph of Arimathea was not a vagabond; he was firmly planted in a geographical location that served as the headquarters for his business empire. One thing that I tell business people or leaders in general is simply this; you cannot

> You can never fulfill the calling of Joseph of Arimathea if you are not rich or super-wealthy.

achieve lasting success if you have a vagabond spirit. You must commit to stay planted in a specific geographical location no matter how successful you become. Obviously, success affords you the ability to have residences in multiple locations but there has to be one geographical beachhead that you will forever hold your loyalty.

Every highly successful person or business had a geographical beginning. Much of the vision and corporate culture of most successful businesses are rooted in understanding the impact the geography their place of origin had on its founders. When Sam Walton began the highly successful multi-billion-dollar chain stores, Wal-Mart, he was domiciled in a small town called Bentonville, Arkansas. Even though the Walton family has made billions of dollars since the founding of the first Wal-Mart store in Bentonville, the corporate headquarters of the company remains Bentonville, Arkansas. Most of the Walton family members still retain Bentonville, Arkansas as their primary residence even though they own houses in other locations as well.

Donald Trump is a multi-billionaire real estate mogul with a vast array of some of the world's most iconic buildings but he is from New York. You can't listen to Donald Trump for a long time without hearing him remind you that he is first and foremost a New Yorker. In his bestselling book The Art of the Deal, Donald Trump is the first one to tell you that he owes much of his current wealth to the City of New York. The City of New York is where he launched his real estate career. Even though the "Donald" has several other residences in the USA, his primary residence is in New York at Trump Tower. New York has essentially been the primary base for his extraordinary wealth.

When Donald Trump was running to become the Republican Presidential nominee, it was his very high margin of victory in the

New York Republican Primary that became the turning point for his presidential campaign that eventually landed him the highly sought after Republican Presidential presumptive nominee status. I have a question for you. What city are you loyal to? What city is the

You cannot achieve lasting success if you have a vagabond spirit.

beginning of your wealth? You should be able to answer these questions without blinking an eye. If you cannot you are in serious trouble of losing sight of the roots and origins of your wealth. This is when you slowly start losing your wealth too! Consequently, the statement, "a rich man from Arimathea," is no insignificant statement. It's a huge and foundational statement that is one of the key ingredients shared by some of the richest people on earth. They all have one special city that bears the root of their present success.

#3 - HIS NAME WAS JOSEPH

*Now when evening had come, there came a rich man from Arimathea, **named Joseph**, who himself had also become a disciple of Jesus.* Matthew 27:57

The third feature about becoming a Joseph of Arimathea in the Kingdom is crystalized in the statement, "there came a rich man from Arimathea, named Joseph." This third feature confronts us with the power of his name. His name was Joseph. This statement might sound simple and obvious. Needless to say, it's an extremely powerful feature and necessary ingredient to becoming a Joseph of Arimathea in God's Kingdom. We have already noted in the first chapter that the first time the name Joseph is mentioned in Scripture it carries a very powerful Hebraic meaning. The name is a literal living prophecy powered by the presence of God. The name Joseph means, *"increase or profits that are divinely inspired or fueled by the power of God."*

In my bestselling and signature book, <u>The Order of Melchizedek</u> I discuss the technology of names. The technology of names is one of the most important spiritual technologies for manifesting dominion and effecting change God ever gave to mankind. Below is a portion of this teaching:

"The angel Gabriel appears one final time in the New Testament to announce the birth of the world's promised Messiah—Jesus. When the angel Gabriel appeared to Joseph in a dream, he told him to call the child who was going to be born out of Mary's womb, Jesus! Jesus means "Savior." These incidences clearly showcase the importance of names in the spiritual realm. An incorrect name can give birth to an inaccurate expression of a person or an entity's intended purpose. *And out of the ground the LORD God formed every beast of the field, and every fowl of the air; and brought them unto Adam to see what he would call them: and whatsoever*

Adam called every living creature, that was the name thereof (Genesis 2:19).

I am afraid that many members of the Body of Christ do not respect the "technology of names" as much as God does. Notwithstanding, this ancient spiritual technology is the method that God uses to determine the capacity, function, and nature of a thing. God imparted this technology of names to Adam. The Bible says that God brought all the animals on earth to Adam to see what he would call or name them. The Bible tells us that whatever name Adam gave to any animal, the name would enshrine that particular animal's purpose, potential, and nature."[4]

The Bible, through the proverbs of Solomon, the richest man who has ever lived, tells us that a good name is more precious than silver and gold. In the United States of America for instance, there is a credit rating system that applies a credit score to a person's name based upon their prior history of making payments on their financial obligations. The higher the credit score the higher the financial borrowing power attached to that particular name. Consequently, if a person's credit score is low it means they don't have a good name before potential creditors because of

The technology of names is one of the most important spiritual technologies for manifesting dominion.

defaulting on previous creditors that appear on such a person's credit report.

I know many God fearing people whose business dreams were shuttered because they couldn't borrow money from reputable lenders to help them launch their business venture: they didn't have a good name as reflected in their credit score. Perhaps this is what the great King Solomon was saying when he said, a "good name is rather to be chosen than silver and gold (Proverbs 22:1)." I have a question for you, "How much value would the business community and financial institutions in your area place on your name?" Do you have a record of borrowing money and then paying  it back to the investors with interest or do you have a reputation of not honoring your financial commitments? Answer these questions prayerfully because it may be at the root of your business failures and the lack of prosperity in your life. Joseph's name also means that he was a man who was comfortable with experiencing increase in everything he touched. Are you ready for increase?

Kingdom entrepreneurs who have already achieved the status of "rich or super-wealthy" must never be ashamed of their social and economic status in life.

#4 - THE POWER OF BECOMING

*Now when evening had come, there came a rich man from Arimathea, named Joseph, **who himself had also become a** disciple of Jesus.* Matthew 27:57

The fourth feature about becoming a Joseph of Arimathea in the Kingdom is crystalized in the statement, "who himself had also become." The statement "who himself had also become" introduces us to one of the most important Kingdom principles governing personal development. The statement gives us two very important facts about Joseph of Arimathea, namely:

1. There was a time in Joseph of Arimathea's life when he was not a disciple of Jesus Christ. He was probably a devout Jew who kept the religious traditions of his forefathers, but he had not yet been introduced to Christ's revolutionary life and message.

2. There came a time in Joseph of Arimathea's life when he was confronted with a life changing decision. The choice to become a disciple of Jesus (Yeshua) or continue following the religious traditions of his forefathers. It's quite clear from the above scriptural passage that he made the right choice. He chose to become a disciple of Jesus.

One of the most important principles governing personal development is the "principle of becoming!" This principle informs us that any person on earth is capable of becoming someone better than they are right now. We don't have to stay the same; we can become better versions of our present self. This statement should be a source of hope for all of us. If a woman is in an abusive relationship with a man she loves, it's only the principle of becoming that can give her a ray of hope that things can turn around for the better. Otherwise the woman would forever be trapped in a hellish relationship with a man incapable of loving her back or treating her like a queen.

I know of business leaders who realized that drinking alcohol was a detriment so they stopped and became better versions of themselves; no longer victims of alcohol. I know of athletes in both the NFL and NBA who realized that certain activities they were doing off the field were bringing down the level of their game on the field of play. They made a conscious choice to remove all the distractions and then went on to become highly successful professional players. When they removed the unnecessary distractions, they became grand masters of their sport of choice.

The principle of becoming lies at the heart of the Gospel of Jesus Christ. If you are a rich or wealthy person and are reading this book but realize that you are not yet a disciple of Jesus; there is still time for you to commit or give your life to the Lord Jesus Christ. Simply stop reading for a few minutes and pray a simple prayer of faith. Open your mouth and ask the Lord Jesus to come and dwell in your heart (Romans 10:11-17). Ask Him to forgive you of all your sins. If you do this now, you will start your spiritual journey of becoming a true and devout disciple of Jesus Christ.

Now Joseph had a dream, and he told it to his brothers; and they hated him even more. So he said to them, "Please hear this dream which I have dreamed: There we were, binding sheaves in the field. Then behold, my sheaf arose and also stood upright; and indeed your sheaves stood all around and bowed down to my sheaf." And his brothers said to him, "Shall you indeed reign over us? Or shall you indeed have dominion over us?" So they hated him even more for his dreams and for his words. (Genesis 37:5-8)

When Joseph, Jacob's son, was young, he was impulsive and lacked discretion. He told his envious brothers every dream God gave him. This impulsiveness and lack of discretion earned him the hatred of his own brothers. They eventually devised a diabolical plan to get rid of the dreamer in the family. Years later when his brothers came to Egypt looking for food, Joseph did not reveal himself to them immediately. Instead, he put them through months of intense testing to see if they too had also become better men. To his pleasant surprise his older brothers had become more caring for each other's welfare, especially that of Joseph's younger brother Benjamin. When Joseph saw this, he was overcome with emotion and revealed himself to his bedazzled brothers. I want you to know that in order for you to embrace the Joseph of Arimathea Calling you must embrace vigorously the power of the principle of becoming!

#5 - A DISCIPLE OF JESUS

*Now when evening had come, there came a rich man from Arimathea, named Joseph, who himself had also become a **disciple of Jesus**. Matthew 27:57*

The fifth feature about becoming a Joseph of Arimathea in the Kingdom is crystalized in the statement, "who himself had also become a disciple of Jesus." Perhaps fewer things in this listing of features are as important as the statement that Joseph of Arimathea became a devout disciple of Jesus. Tell me who is mentoring you or whose counsel you follow and I will tell you your future. You are only as good as the quality of the voices that speak into your life. When you become a disciple of someone you

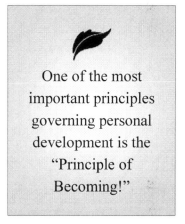

One of the most important principles governing personal development is the "Principle of Becoming!"

effectively make his or her voice the predominant voice of authority in your life. It won't be long before you start patterning your life after him or her.

Mentorship (fathering) is important. It decides whose voice and principles you follow. The Scripture tells us that Joseph of Arimathea had become a "disciple of Jesus." This means that Joseph of Arimathea was being mentored or fathered spiritually by the Lord Jesus Christ. When it comes to mentors and authority figures, Joseph of Arimathea had certainly chosen well. Who can be a better spiritual mentor than the Lord Jesus Christ? What lifestyle is better emulating than the life of the Lord Jesus Christ? The mission, Kingdom principles, and concepts that Jesus taught while He was on earth seriously influenced a disciple, by name of Joseph of Arimathea. Joseph of Arimathea was obviously in love with Jesus, His mission, and the establishment of His Kingdom here on earth. This would explain why Joseph of Arimathea couldn't resist going to see Pontus Pilate to rescue the lifeless body of Jesus! He was a true love-ravished disciple of Jesus Christ of Nazareth.

Most importantly there is another added dimension to the statement, "who himself had also become a disciple of Jesus." This statement flies in the face of religious leaders who erroneously teach that it is more difficult for a rich man to enter the Kingdom of God than for a camel to go through the eye of a needle. Joseph of Arimathea was a very rich man and who was just as much a disciple of Jesus as he was rich. His immense wealth did not diminish the passion of his discipleship by one iota. It's true that money only enhances what a person already is: if a person is inherently crooked, having more money will only increase opportunities for him to be crooked. On the other hand, if someone is very decent and generous, having more money will only increase his or her ability to be more philanthropic. God wants to raise highly successful Kingdom entrepreneurs who are also serious disciples of Jesus Christ.

#6 - A MAN OF PROMINENCE

*Now when evening had come, because it was the Preparation Day, that is, the day before the Sabbath, Joseph of Arimathea, **a prominent council member**, who was himself waiting for the kingdom of God, coming and taking courage, went in to Pilate and asked for the body of Jesus.* Mark 15:42-43

The sixth feature about becoming a Joseph of Arimathea in the Kingdom is crystalized in the statement, "Joseph of Arimathea, a prominent council member." This sixth feature informs us of the fact that not only was Joseph of Arimathea rich; he was also a man of prominence in Jewish society. The Bible tells us that he was a prominent council member. I believe that the council he was on was either the influential Sanhedrin council or a similar political action committee. Either way the Holy Spirit did not want us to miss the importance of his prominence in society. I am almost convinced that it

Tell me who is mentoring you or whose counsel you follow and I will tell you your future. You are only as good as the quality of the voices that speak into your life.

was Joseph of Arimathea's coveted position on the Sanhedrin council that brought him into contact with Pontus Pilate, Governor of Rome. Maybe they met at some high level social gathering but my money is on the Sanhedrin council. The Sanhedrin council did a lot of political negotiations with Rome on behalf of the Jewish people.

It is important to note that there is a critical difference between being rich and being prominent in society. The Strong's Concordance uses the Greek word (eusx?mon) for the word "prominent" used in the above passage of scripture to refer to "Joseph of Arimathea." The Greek word (eusx?mon) is used in Koine Greek of a person who properly uses influence, especially by serving in a high (respected) position. Being rich means having easy access to capital to finance whatever you want to buy. On the other hand, prominence also means having a position(s) of influence in society. Obviously, there are some very prominent politicians in most countries who are not rich; but their voice commands respect in society. Needless to say, when someone is both rich and prominent in society, as Joseph of Arimathea was, is truly a double barreled gun. This means that Joseph of Arimathea was the kind of man who could engage you from either the wealth side or the prominence side of his life's portfolio. This is why I encourage every person reading this book who senses the "Joseph of Arimathea Calling" upon their life to begin to consider running for prominent positions on certain councils or boards of organizations that are deeply entrenched in the community. You never know when your position of influence on a certain board or council is the difference between the Kingdom advancing or going backwards.

#7 - SOLD OUT TO THE GOSPEL OF THE KINGDOM

Joseph of Arimathea, a prominent council member, who was **himself waiting for the Kingdom of God**, *coming and taking courage, went in to Pilate and asked for the body of Jesus.* Mark 15:43

The seventh feature about becoming a Joseph of Arimathea in the Kingdom is crystalized in the statement, 'who was himself waiting for the Kingdom of God." I love this seventh feature of becoming a Joseph of Arimathea, because it proves above all others that Joseph of Arimathea was truly a disciple of Jesus. As they say, the "proof is in the pudding". According to the late Dr. Myles Munroe, the number one message of Jesus Christ that most Christian churches hardly ever teach today is the "Gospel of the Kingdom." Most Christian business people are simply that, Christians in business but the Body of Christ has very few true Kingdom entrepreneurs. I hope and pray that this book will help increase the number of true Kingdom entrepreneurs in the global Body of Christ. A Christian businessman is a man whose livelihood is found in the business arena and who maintains control of his sphere of influence. A Kingdom entrepreneur, on the other hand, is a business owner who has relinquished control of said business enterprise to the King of kings. These Kingdom entrepreneurs have voluntarily relinquished control of their business and made Jesus the true CEO to use it as a vehicle for advancing the Kingdom here on earth. Which one are you?

The Gospel of the Kingdom is the most predominant message Jesus Christ ever taught (Matthew 6:33). This is because the Lord Jesus knew that Adam and Eve did not lose a religion in the Garden, they lost a Kingdom. Since the fall of man, mankind has been in search of rediscovering the Kingdom. Jesus knew this; thus, it is what He mostly talked about. If Joseph of Arimathea was a true disciple of Jesus Christ, we will find the same exact passion for the manifestation of the Kingdom here on earth as it was in the heart of Jesus. We need look no further than the statement, "who was himself waiting for the Kingdom of God." Joseph of Arimathea, like the other disciples who were with Jesus, was looking for the arrival of the Kingdom of God. Below is a statement made by Dr. Myles Munroe, which will help you discern the critical difference between religion and the Gospel of the Kingdom, as Jesus preached it.

In his bestselling book, Rediscovering the Kingdom Dr. Myles Munroe says the following, "The power of religion lies in its ability to serve as a substitute for the Kingdom and thus hinder humankind from pursuing the genuine answer to man's dilemma. My study of the nature of religion and how it impacts the process of man's search for the Kingdom uncovered several significant truths:

- Religion preoccupies man until he finds the Kingdom.
- Religion is what man does until he finds the Kingdom.
- Religion prepares man to leave earth; the Kingdom empowers man to dominate the earth.

- Religion is reaching up to God; the Kingdom is God coming down to man.

- Religion wants to escape the earth; the Kingdom impacts, influences and changes earth.

- Religion seeks to take earth to Heaven; the Kingdom seeks to bring Heaven to earth.'"?[5]

#8 - A MAN OF COURAGE

*Joseph of Arimathea, a prominent council member, who was himself waiting for the kingdom of God, **coming and taking courage**, went in to Pilate and asked for the body of Jesus. Mark 15:43*

The eighth feature about becoming a Joseph of Arimathea in the Kingdom is found in the expression, "coming and taking courage." Courage is colorless and transcends nationality but when you see it you can't ignore it. Most importantly courage is not the absence of fear; it's acting on behalf of the greater good in face of one's fears. Why would the Holy Spirit use the word courage to describe what Joseph of Arimathea did on that fateful day? We must remember that there was no subject that was more mired in a highly heated political and

God wants to raise highly successful kingdom entrepreneurs who are also serious disciples of Jesus Christ.

religious controversy like the death and crucifixion of Jesus of Nazareth. The political and spiritual atmosphere in Jerusalem was so volatile you would be endangering your very life if you happened to identify yourself with Jesus of Nazareth.

Because of this volatile atmosphere Peter denied Jesus three times to hide their close association. However, it was in such an explosive spiritual and political climate that Joseph of Arimathea found the courage to risk it all to rescue the body of Jesus. I both envy and admire Joseph of Arimathea at the same time. I wish I was the one who had been given the opportunity to rescue the body of Jesus. It is apparent that those who walk in the Joseph of Arimathea calling must also be graced and willing to operate

"Courage is not the absence of fear; it's acting on behalf of the greater good in face of one's fears."

in courage in order to face the potential persecution that accompanies it. There is nothing more pitiful than prominent, wealthy, but cowardly disciples who will not speak up or stand for what they believe in when it matters most.

The cancer of cowardly leadership in American society may help explain why millions of Americans have fallen in love with a politically incorrect talker like Donald J. Trump in the 2016 Presidential election cycle. They see him as someone who is willing to say what he thinks no matter the cost to his political ambitions.

While I believe that the most effective way of operating in the marketplace is in stealth mode there comes a moment in time when Kingdom entrepreneurs must make known their complete allegiance to God's Kingdom, no matter the cost to themselves. Pontius Pilate or Caiaphas the high priest could have easily ordered the execution of Joseph of Arimathea for making such an unusual request. They could have accused him of treason. Nevertheless, Joseph of Arimathea took courage and was determined not to allow his fear of persecution or prosecution to get in the way of rescuing the body of Jesus.

#9 - LEVERAGING
STRATEGIC POLITICAL ALLIANCES

*Joseph of Arimathea, a prominent council member, who was himself waiting for the kingdom of God, coming and taking courage, **went in to Pilate** and asked for the body of Jesus. Pilate marveled that He was already dead; and summoning the centurion, he asked him if He had been dead for some time. So when he found out from the centurion, he granted the body to Joseph.* Mark 15:43-45

The ninth characteristic reflected in Joseph of Arimathea in the Kingdom is found in the statement, "went in to Pilate and asked for the body of Jesus." This Joseph of Arimathea brings us into deep waters, the arena of politics. It is quite clear from the above statement that is impossible for anyone to fully embrace the Joseph of

Arimathea calling without forming strategic alliances with other influencers in the political arena. As previously stated, the church cannot afford to look at politics as a dirty game or something they are to steer clear of anymore. The reality is staggeringly simple; there is no nation on earth that is not impacted by the prevailing political atmosphere within its borders. The global Body of Christ cannot expect to exercise its godly influence over the nations if it remains in a political vacuum. Whether we like it or not the Body of Christ must not only engage the political arena but needs to also become a breeding ground of Kingdom minded Daniel type politicians.

Ask yourself the question, "Why did Joseph of Arimathea find it quite easy to get an audience with Pontius Pilate, Governor of Rome?" The answer is obvious; they were already connected politically through Joseph's many business dealings. His business activities and political acumen had already given him a political foothold with the governor of Rome. Another equally important question to ask ourselves, "Why would Pontius Pilate place his political career in jeopardy by granting his strange request?" At that time in Palestine, there was nobody who was surrounded by more political and religious controversy than Jesus Christ of Nazareth. Granting the body of Jesus to Joseph of Arimathea was no small task since both the Sanhedrin Council and King Herod were interested in what happened to the body of Jesus.

The Sanhedrin Council probably wanted to cremate the body of Jesus to stop His resurrection and avoid a religious insurrection that the resurrection of Jesus would cause in Israel. King Herod on the other hand wanted Jesus to stay dead to avoid a political rebellion that the resurrection of Jesus would cause in Israel. I have been around enough politicians to know that no matter what the country or party, politicians are basically the same: they operate by "what's in it for me or what have you done for me lately" mentality. In other words, they only help people who give them an advantage politically or have donated to their political campaigns in times past. I believe that Pontius Pilate was no different. Kingdom entrepreneurs must be masterful in discovering legal and ethical avenues for using money to win friends and influence people in the political arena without crossing the line. Having positive relationships with politicians can be a great asset to Kingdom businesspeople that can be leveraged to give an advantage to the Kingdom of God. Jesus talked about the strategy of using money to win or make friends (Luke 16:9). Unfortunately, the Body of Christ has not used this strategy effectively to its advantage. We will discuss this strategy in more details in a later chapter

#10 - RESCUING THE BODY OF JESUS

*Joseph of Arimathea, a prominent council member, who was himself waiting for the kingdom of God, coming and taking courage, went in to Pilate and **asked for the body of Jesus**.* Mark 15:43

The tenth feature about becoming a Joseph of Arimathea in the Kingdom is identified in the statement, "and asked for the body of Jesus!" This tenth feature about becoming a Joseph of Arimathea leaves me teary eyed. This tenth feature about becoming a "Joseph of Arimathea," is the primary reason why Joseph of Arimathea risked his life, business career, and social status in the Jewish community. He simply wanted to rescue the body of Jesus at whatever cost to himself! For lack of a better word; his was a rescue mission, and the objective was to get the body of Jesus Christ of

The Church cannot afford to look at politics as a "dirty game" anymore.

Nazareth under his control. I will ask this question again, it's worth repeating here. "What Kingdom assignment would be more important for any Kingdom businessperson than to rescue the body of Jesus Christ of Nazareth?"

This tenth feature also exemplifies the true and highest calling of any Joseph of Arimathea; that is to rescue the Body of Christ. God is going to use the ministry of His wealthy disciples in the nations of the world to rescue the Body of Christ (Christians) from demonically engineered political and religious persecution. This is what I call "money with a mission!".

#11 - CAN GOD TRUST
YOU WITH THE BODY OF CHRIST?

*When Joseph **had taken the body**, he wrapped it in a clean linen cloth, and laid it in his new tomb, which he had hewn out of the rock; and he rolled a large stone against the door of the tomb, and departed.* Matthew 27:59-60

The eleventh feature about becoming a Joseph of Arimathea in the kingdom is found in the statement, "When Joseph had taken the body, he wrapped it in a clean linen cloth, and laid it in his new tomb." This statement gives me goosebumps. What physical asset could be more priceless than the lifeless body of the world's long awaited Messiah? For centuries, the prophets of old, under the inspiration of the Holy Spirit, prophesied about the coming of a righteous branch (the Messiah) who would save the world from the law of sin and death. There has not been an entrance of a child into this world, which was more highly anticipated than the supernatural birth of the Lord Jesus Christ.

My favorite scripture concerning the arrival of the world's promised Messiah is Hebrews 10:5. "Therefore, when He came into the world, He said: "Sacrifice and offering you did not desire, but a body you have prepared for Me." We are told that God was not interested in animal sacrifices and offerings, but rather He was interested in the special physical body of flesh that was prepared to do His will. Without inhabiting the body of Jesus, Christ (the Living Word) would have had no legal way of redeeming us from the power

127

of sin and the devil. Thus, the flesh body of Jesus that Joseph of Arimathea was entrusted to protect was also the priceless body of the Christ.

This point brings me to why this feature of the Joseph of Arimathea calling leaves with me goosebumps: God almighty in His eternal wisdom entrusted the lifeless body of His only begotten Son into the hands of a rich and prominent businessman, Joseph of Arimathea. The Lord showed me that He is not looking to produce Kingdom entrepreneurs who are simply wealthy. He wants to produce Kingdom entrepreneurs who, like Joseph of Arimathea can be trusted to handle the Body of Christ with tender care. Unfortunately, many wealthy followers of Christ are using their wealth to manipulate pastors and control the Body of Christ. This grieves the Holy Spirit. I know of a senior pastor of a large church who was given an ultimatum by one of his wealthy church members. The man told this pastor that if he did not do what he wanted, he would stop supporting the church financially. He would also tell other business people in the church to do the same. This is so sad. This rich brother was no Joseph of Arimathea. He represents that segment of wealthy Christians who grieve and offend the Holy Ghost by using the power of their wealth to manipulate the Body of Christ. This is not to say that pastors should not listen to the wise financial counsel of some of their prominent business leaders: only a foolish and prideful pastor will ignore the wise and godly counsel of a true Joseph of Arimathea that God has planted in his or her church.

#12 - PRESERVING THE BODY OF CHRIST

*When Joseph had taken the body, **he wrapped it in a clean linen cloth,** and laid it in his new tomb, which he had hewn out of the rock; and he rolled a large stone against the door of the tomb, and departed.* Matthew 27:59-60

The twelfth feature about becoming a Joseph of Arimathea in the kingdom is crystalized in the statement, "When Joseph had taken the body, he wrapped it in a clean linen cloth, and laid it in his new tomb." This statement presents us with another very interesting dynamic of the Joseph of Arimathea calling. This feature deals with using one's wealth to preserve the Body of Christ. The Bible and biblical historians both agree that Jesus was so severely beaten, that it was difficult to even recognize His face while He hung on the cross. It goes without saying that when Joseph of Arimathea secured the bloodied body of Jesus, he had to do a lot of work to prepare it for burial. In keeping with the burial customs of most wealthy people of Jesus' day I am almost certain that Joseph of Arimathea had a team of experts who applied the best essentials oils for preserving a dead body that was only available to people of means in society. True to Isaiah's prophecy, Joseph of Arimathea made it possible for Jesus to be "numbered with the rich in His death' (Isaiah 53)!

The Holy Spirit, said to me, "Son I am looking for Kingdom entrepreneurs who will use their vast wealth to preserve the Body of Christ." The Bible tells us "when Joseph had taken the body, he wrapped it in a clean linen cloth." The clean linen cloth that Joseph of Arimathea provided our Lord and Savior is what is now famously known as the "Shroud of Turin." The Shroud of Turin is the most revered article in Catholicism. It is rumored to contain the bloody imprint of the face of Jesus. "How and where are you using your wealth to preserve the Body of Christ?"

#13 - BANKROLLING: THE BODY OF CHRIST

So when he found out from the centurion, he granted the body to Joseph. ***Then he bought fine linen,*** *took Him down, and wrapped Him in the linen. And he laid Him in a tomb which had been hewn out of the rock, and rolled a stone against the door of the tomb.* Mark 15:45-46

The thirteenth feature about becoming a Joseph of Arimathea in the kingdom is evident in the statement, "Then he bought fine linen, took Him down, and wrapped Him in the linen." This aspect of the Joseph of Arimathea calling presents us with the solution as to "what we should be doing with our money." There is absolutely nothing more dangerous than money without a divinely inspired mission. Money needs to be deployed behind a divinely inspired mission or the deceitfulness of riches will destroy the souls of those who have it! This aspect of the Joseph of Arimathea calling shows that the true purpose of money is to bankroll the Body of Christ. The Bible tells us that Joseph of Arimathea bought fine linen, fitting of royalty, so he could dress the naked body of Jesus. The expression "bought fine linen" clearly indicates that moving the body of Jesus, cleaning it, preparing it for burial with very expensive essential oils cost Joseph of Arimathea a fortune. Joseph of Arimathea became the bank for a dead man (Jesus), who was incapable of making His own burial arrangements!

Across the nations of the world, the wind of the Spirit is blowing from the marketplace to the temple. God is raising men and women like Joseph of Arimathea who will not hesitate to bankroll the needs of the Body of Christ as well as the costs of evangelizing the world. These men and women will pump millions of dollars into the propagation of the Gospel of Jesus Christ and for the discipleship of nations. The work of these end-time Kingdom wealth masters in financing the advancement of the Kingdom is just as important as of the work of notable evangelists who stand in front of millions of souls and make the call for salvation. Without the wealth and generosity of these Joseph of Arimathea's, global evangelization will come to a screeching halt. Romans 10 tells

Unfortunately, many wealthy followers of Christ are using their wealth to manipulate pastors and control the Body of Christ.

us, *"How can they (unbelievers) hear (the Gospel) unless someone is sent?"* The wealth of these Joseph of Arimathea's will cause thousands of evangelists and missionaries to hit the streets running. "Are you ready to become a Kingdom paymaster to help spread the Gospel of Jesus Christ more rapidly than it is currently spreading?" I hope and pray that your answer to this question is a resounding, heartfelt "Yes!!!"

#14 - NUMBERED WITH THE RICH IN DEATH

When Joseph had taken the body, he wrapped it in a clean linen cloth, **and laid it in his new tomb, which he had hewn out of the rock**; *and he rolled a large stone against the door of the tomb, and departed.* Matthew 27:59-60

The fourteenth aspect about becoming a Joseph of Arimathea in the Kingdom is crystalized in the statement, "when Joseph had taken the body, he wrapped it in a clean linen cloth, and laid it in his new tomb, which he had hewn out of the rock; and he rolled a large stone against the door of the tomb, and departed." This final aspect of the Joseph of Arimathea calling is truly fascinating. This aspect of the Joseph of Arimathea calling unites the power of wealth with the power of prophecy to fulfill the eternal purposes of God. This final feature of the Joseph of Arimathea calling is what makes Kingdom entrepreneurs become what I call "Prophecy Fulfillers!"

More than 1000 years before the supernatural virgin birth of the Lord Jesus Christ, a Jewish prophet, Isaiah, son of Amoz, was moved by the Spirit to prophesy, *"And they made His grave with the wicked—But with the rich at His death, because He had done no violence, nor was any deceit in His mouth"* (Isaiah 53:9). For over 1000 years it appears this messianic prophecy was spoken out of tune.

It looked like it would never be fulfilled. What gave this prophecy ultimate importance is that the prophecy was about a Messiah; the Seed of the woman (Genesis 3:14-15) who was destined to save God's creation from the penalty of sin and death.

It looked like the ancient messianic prophecy that was floating from one generation to the next, would never find a time of divine fulfillment. Thankfully, God is so very faithful. In His eternal foreknowledge God had already raised a rich man by the name of Joseph of Arimathea who was anointed as a "Prophecy Fulfiller!" His vast wealth and political influence would allow Isaiah's prophecy to find a home. Isaiah's prophecy declares that the Messiah (Yeshua/Jesus) would "be numbered with the rich in death!" How is this possible? On the cross Jesus was crucified with the wicked (the two thieves on the cross) and yet in death (burial), He would be numbered with the rich. How? The only way this prophecy makes sense is when we remember what Joseph of Arimathea did for the lifeless body of Jesus. He took it from the cross, washed it, prepped it with very costly essential oils, dressed it in fine (very expensive) linen and then buried it a tomb that only the wealthy in Israel could afford. In so doing Joseph of Arimathea, whether he knew it or not fulfilled the age-old prophecy. The power of Joseph of Arimathea's wealth collided with the power of prophecy and the result was divine fulfillment!

The Holy Ghost is showing me that God is raising men and women all over the world who carry the mantle of Joseph of Arimathea. This prophetic company of Kingdom entrepreneurs is going to allow the power of their wealth to fuse with the eternal power of prophecy. Many of the checks they will write to bankroll a church, ministry or Kingdom project will result in the fulfillment of someone else's prophecy that they have been waiting on God to fulfill. Several months ago, a well-respected prophet of God told me that God was going to use an African businessman to sow one million South African Rand into my ministry to demonstrate to me that God was going to use my ministry mightily in Africa, even though I am based in the United States. Recently, I was teaching about Joseph of Arimathea to a group of South African businessmen, when one of the businessmen was so moved by my teaching that he told everyone in the audience that God

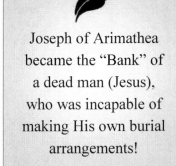

Joseph of Arimathea became the "Bank" of a dead man (Jesus), who was incapable of making His own burial arrangements!

was telling him to sow one million ZAR into my ministry. I was speechless; because this was the single largest donation ever pledged to our ministry in Africa! The pledged donation was equivalent to about sixty thousand US dollars. Without knowing it this Kingdom entrepreneur became a "Prophecy Fulfiller!"

PONTIUS PILATE:
BUILDING STRATEGIC POLITICAL ALLIANCES

Politics is a dirty game. How many times have you heard that expression fall from the lips of Christian leaders and Christians in general? Taken literally it sends a very chilling message. It sends the message that Christians are not supposed to be involved in politics This kind of foolish thinking is the reason the church has had very little influence in the public square. And yet politics is at the center of governance of every country where Christians live. How dumb is this? How can we exclude ourselves from participating in the political process when Jesus clearly tells us that we are both salt and light? This dangerous expression "politics is a dirty game," must be put to rest before it sentences the church into the corridors of cultural irrelevancy.

Joseph of Arimathea, a prominent council member, who was himself waiting for the kingdom of God, coming and taking courage, went in to Pilate and asked for the body of Jesus.

Pilate marveled that He was already dead; and summoning the centurion, he asked him if He had been dead for some time. So when he found out from the centurion, he granted the body to Joseph. Mark 15:43-45

In the previous chapter, we discussed 14 unique features of the Joseph of Arimathea Calling. The ninth feature about becoming a Joseph of Arimathea in the Kingdom of God is crystalized in the statement, *"went in to Pilate and asked for the body of Jesus. Pilate marveled that He was already dead; and summoning the centurion, he asked him if He had been dead for some time. So when he found out from the centurion, he granted the body to Joseph."* As I stated previously, this ninth feature about becoming a Joseph of Arimathea truly brings us into deep waters, the arena of politics. It is quite clear from the statement above that it is impossible for anyone to fully embrace the Joseph of Arimathea calling without forming strategic alliances with politicians in the political arena. I will be repeating some things I have already mentioned in the previous chapters because they are of such importance in understanding how we can engage the political arena as people of faith.

As previously stated, the Body of Christ can no longer afford to look at politics as a dirty game that they are supposed to stay away from at all costs. You can never talk of fundamentally reforming nations without bringing the spirit of reformation to the political process. The prevailing political atmosphere in any nation matters to business and social issues. If there is political upheaval that turns violent, like what happened in Rwanda, the Church cannot afford to sit on the sidelines. The political upheaval in Rwanda between the Hutu and Tutsi led to the genocide of over one million innocent people! Many of the victims of this bloody genocide were God-fearing Christians. So much for the "politics is a dirty game" we are not supposed to be involved in. The Body of Christ cannot expect to exercise its godly influence over the nations unless it engages in the political process. Change does not occur in a vacuum. As distasteful as we may find politics we must not only engage in the political process it must become a training ground for Kingdom minded Daniel-type

This dangerous expression, "politics is a dirty game" must be put to rest before it sentences the church into the corridors of cultural irrelevancy.

politicians that the church must embrace and support. Daniel was deeply entrenched in the politics and political system of Babylon where he was domiciled. In fact, he and his other three Hebrew brothers are a testament to the positive impact that people of faith can exert on the politics of their countries of residence.

It was through his business dealings that Joseph of Arimathea became connected with Pontius Pilate. His business dealings and political acumen had already given him a political foothold with the governor of Rome. Additionally, all political treaties between Rome and its Jewish subjects were negotiated through the very powerful

Sanhedrin Council. Joseph of Arimathea was a prominent member of this Jewish political action committee.

I would daresay that it was Jesus' teaching on the Kingdom of God that caused religious and political leaders to conspire against Him more so than His teaching on the love of God. In other words, it was His impact on their political power more so than their religious standing that men feared most. This is why granting the body of Jesus to Joseph of Arimathea was no small task, considering the fact that both the Sanhedrin Council and King Herod were both very much interested in what happened to the body. None of them wanted the body of Jesus to be used in a political and religious conspiracy. Both entities, the political and religious, wanted to put to an end to the Jesus Revolution, which was rocking the City of Jerusalem. The Jesus Revolution was also threatening the power of political and religious establishments.

I have been around enough politicians to know that politicians are basically the same globally. They are creatures of survival and operate by the mantra "what is in it for me or what have you done for me lately." In other words, for the most part, politicians only help people who give them an advantage politically or have donated to their political campaigns in times past. I believe that Pontius Pilate was no different. Kingdom entrepreneurs must discover legal avenues to use money to win friends in the political arena without going into the realm of evil bribes. Politicians are great assets to have in your toolbox as a Kingdom businessperson that you can leverage in the evil day to give an advantage to the Kingdom of God. Jesus talked about the strategy of using money to win or make friends in the sixteenth chapter of the Gospel of Luke. Unfortunately, the Body of Christ has not used this strategy effectively to its advantage. We will discuss this strategy in more details in the last chapter of this book.

And I tell you [learn from this], make friends for yourselves [for eternity] by means of the wealth of unrighteousness [that is, use material resources as a way to further the work of God], so that when it runs out, they will welcome you into the eternal dwellings. Luke 16:9 Amplified Bible

THE KINGDOM OF GOD AND POLITICS

While I believe that the church can no longer sit on the sidelines, politically speaking, there is a balancing act between advancing the Kingdom of God and our involvement in the political process. One of the greatest dangers of Christian political activism is that many born again believers confuse it with the work of advancing the Kingdom of God. This is a toxic error in need of a careful and surgical course correction. The confusion between the work of the Kingdom and Christian political activism is rooted in the fact that many well-meaning born-again believers do not understand the dynamics of their dual citizenship. Understanding how this dual citizenship affects Kingdom citizens in the political process is the key to affecting the needed course correction.

139

Saint Paul makes it very clear that every born again believer is first and foremost a citizen of the Kingdom of Heaven. (Philippians 3:20.) As Kingdom citizens, our primary responsibility is to preach the Gospel of the Kingdom so that the hearts of sinners can be transformed by the saving knowledge of Jesus Christ. This is how the Kingdom of God is advanced in the earth, heart-to-heart, spirit-to-spirit. The Kingdom of God can never be advanced through a political process; to the contrary, trying to advance the Kingdom of God through a political process diminishes the complete sovereignty of the Kingdom of God in the affairs of men. God never asked for a popular vote when He decided to temporarily remove King Nebuchadnezzar from the Babylonian throne (Daniel 4:28-35). The Kingdom of God is too

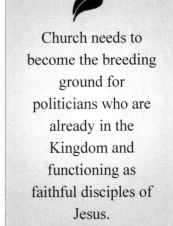

Church needs to become the breeding ground for politicians who are already in the Kingdom and functioning as faithful disciples of Jesus.

powerful to be quarantined in a man-made political process. Since the Kingdom of God cannot be advanced through a political process, how then is it advanced? It is forcefully advanced through transformed hearts displaying the power, signs and wonders of the Kingdom of God in the ministry, marketplace and municipality. This is how Joseph, Daniel and the Apostle Paul advanced the Kingdom of God. (Romans 15:18-19.)

Jesus Christ, the head of the church, made it very clear that the Kingdom of God is not of this world and as such it can never be advanced through the ballot boxes. He had this press conference on the Kingdom and politics in front of Pontius Pilate. He told Pontius Pilate that had His Kingdom been of this world, He would have attempted to deliver Himself through a political process or military campaign. He even rebuked Peter during His arrest in the Garden of Gethsemane for using violence to advance His Kingdom.

When Pilate heard this, he was more frightened than ever. He took Jesus back into the headquarters again and asked him, "Where are you from?" But Jesus gave no answer. "Why don't you talk to me?" Pilate demanded. "Don't you realize that I have the power to release you or crucify you?" Then Jesus said, "You would have no power over me at all unless it were given to you from above. So the one who handed me over to you has the greater sin." John 19:8-11

Now you might say to me, "Francis, are you suggesting that Kingdom citizens are not supposed to be involved in the politics of their nation?" The answer is an emphatic "NO!" This is not what I am suggesting. This is where the dual citizenship of Kingdom citizens comes into play. As naturalized citizens of their countries of residence, Kingdom citizens have a civic duty and moral obligation to politic for the election of political candidates who are most friendly to the core values of the Kingdom of God. Better still, the Church needs to become the breeding ground for politicians who are already in the Kingdom and functioning as faithful disciples of Jesus. But such politicking must never be confused with the work of advancing the Kingdom, even though such politicking is largely influenced by the moral values and worldview of the Kingdom citizen so engaged. Such politicking must be seen for what it is: the civic duty of all good and moral citizens (Romans 13).

For those of us who live in the United States of America, politicking for the Republican or the Democratic Party, must never be confused with the work of advancing the Kingdom of God. The Kingdom of God can work through both political parties and yet it transcends both of them. The Kingdom of God must never be compromised by its citizens to the degree that it is brought under the jurisdiction of unsaved politicians with questionable political agendas. I have seen vicious slander take place between Kingdom citizens (brothers and sisters in Christ) who were politicking for opposing sides. Kingdom citizens must never treat each other like enemies in order to advance any political agenda. When children of God are in involved in politics in opposition parties, they must treat each other with respect, even though they don't see eye-to-eye in their politics. Nevertheless, all things considered, God is raising men and women in the Body of Christ, with a Joseph of Arimathea calling who will actively engage the political arena. God is giving this "Joseph Company" divine wisdom in how to be active politically without drinking from the streams of corruption.

7M STRATEGY FOR TRANSFORMING TODAY'S MARKETPLACE

Here is the mind which has wisdom: The seven heads are seven mountains on which the woman sits. Revelation 17:9

IT IS IMPORTANT THAT THOSE with a Joseph of Arimathea calling understand the concept of the Seven Mountains of Culture (also referred to as the Seven Mountains of Influence) because all those called to the marketplace will do so from one of these mountains. You will have major influence on one mountain but will also interact or be affected by all the other mountains. The Church has focused on one mountain (the Mountain of Religion), totally ignoring the other six mountains where people spend the majority of their time. For those in the marketplace, it is critical to know to which mountain you have been assigned and seek the Lord for strategies that will enable you to conquer and/or strongly influence that mountain. While banished to

143

the island of Patmos the Apostle John was given one of the most powerful revelatory insights into the spiritual structure of Babylon. John saw this ancient demonic system, which looks like a "woman sitting on a scarlet beast full of names of blasphemy" (Revelation 17:1-5). When the Apostle John saw this powerful prophetic vision he quickly noticed that this demonic spirit and system sat on seven spiritual mountains. John, the beloved, saw that the spirit of Babylon rules the whole world by controlling seven strategic mountains. It does not take a rocket scientist to figure out that whoever controls these seven strategic mountains can change the course of nations.

These seven strategic mountains represent seven spiritual kingdoms or systems, which control the affairs of all the nations. These seven mountains that John saw are spiritual mountain-kingdoms which manifest themselves on an earthly plane. Since they are spiritual mountains they can be manipulated by either divine or diabolical activity in the spiritual realm. The purpose of this chapter is to show how every child of God (especially Kingdom entrepreneurs) can function in these seven mountain-kingdoms in order to advance the Kingdom of God here on earth. The call of being a Joseph of Arimathea in God's Kingdom will not be complete without an understanding of how to successfully navigate the ever-changing configurations of these seven mountains or cultural molders. If you are called to function as a Joseph of Arimathea in the Body of Christ, you will most likely create your wealth on one of these seven mountains. It's important to know the mountain(s) that God is calling you to conquer.

The concept of the Seven Mountains of Culture was first revealed to Dr. Bill Bright of Campus Crusades in 1975. Dr. Johnny Enlow and Dr. Lance Wallnau are the most well-known proponents and teachers on the Seven Mountains of Culture. The names that have been given to these seven spiritual mountains or systems, upon which the great whore of Babylon sits are as follows...

1. The Mountain of Finance
2. The Mountain of Business
3. The Mountain of Law & Government
4. The Mountain of Media, Arts and Entertainment
5. The Mountain of Education
6. The Mountain of Family
7. The Mountain of Religion

As God's eternal Kingdom agenda plays itself out through yielded citizens of the Kingdom, Jesus Christ will soon become the Mighty One who controls all the functionality of the seven mountains that the demonic spirit called Babylon the Great currently sits upon. As Kingdom citizens conquer these seven spiritual kingdoms or systems they will then become the domains of God and of His Christ as our gift to God! This is why rather than focus on how God's people can take individuals into the Kingdom of God; we will focus our attention on how God's people can bring these seven mountain into divine alignment with the Kingdom of God. If we can bring these seven spiritual mountains or systems under subjection to God's authority, we will begin to see entire nations turn to God. At the very least the governing influence of God's Kingdom will increase over the affairs of nations.

THE MOUNTAIN OF LAW & GOVERNMENT

We know that the law is good when used correctly. For the law was not intended for people who do what is right. It is for people who are lawless and rebellious, who are ungodly and sinful, who consider nothing sacred and defile what is holy, who kill their father or mother or commit other murders.
1 Timothy 1:8-9

Of the Seven Mountains of Culture my favorite one is the "Mountain of Law & Government." I believe that if the Body of Christ does not take this mountain seriously, influencing the culture and destiny of nations with the culture and principles of the Kingdom of God will be a dismal failure. Below is a quote that I took from one of my favorite books on law and liberty.

"The authority of any system of thought is the god of that system. Men, by denying God, cannot escape God. God is the inescapable reality, and the inescapable category of thought. When men deny the one true God, they do it only to make false gods. Behind every system of Law is a god. To find the

146

god in any system, locate the source of law in that system. If the source of law is the individual, then the individual is the god of that system. If the source of law is the people, or dictatorship of the proletariat, then these things are the gods of those systems. If our source of law is the court, then the court is our god. If there is no higher law beyond man, then man is his own god, or else his creatures, the institutions he has made, have become his gods. When you choose your authority, you choose your god, and where you look for your law, there is your god."[6]

When I read the above quote, I was deeply stirred by the far-reaching spiritual implications of this incredible body of thought. I became doubly convinced that if the Body of Christ does not map out practical strategies to take over or influence the Mountain of Law and Government in their countries of citizenship it will lose the culture war. Please meditate on this phrase, "Behind every system of law is a god. To find the god in any system, locate the source of law in that system." Who is the god behind the system of law and government in your country? It is important you find out, because if the god behind the system of law and government in your country is not Jesus Christ or a Judaic-Christian philosophy;

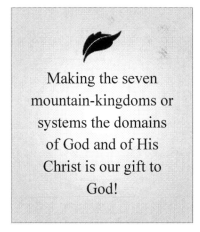

Making the seven mountain-kingdoms or systems the domains of God and of His Christ is our gift to God!

then you just unmasked the demonic principality that you must contend with to win the culture war in your nation. Without a shadow of doubt, the Mountain of Law and Government is the most powerful of the all the seven mountains. You can never become a true Joseph of Arimathea without becoming skilled at navigating the edicts that proceed from the Mountain of Law and Government that have a direct impact on the marketplace. Therefore, all Joseph of Arimathea's must look for ways to lobby politicians to pass laws that do not devastate the economy.

THE MOUNTAIN OF FINANCE

Another of the seven spiritual mountains is the Mountain of Finance. For the most part, the spirit of Babylon (demonic philosophy) controls this mountain. This may explain why fighting for capital (money) to monetize your business idea may be one of the greatest challenges you will ever face. The good news is that the Lord Jesus Christ paid the price on the cross for God's children to experience financial prosperity. Since the Mountain of Finance is a spiritual mountain it can be manipulated by activities taking place in the realm of the spirit. These spiritual activities could either be divinely orchestrated or diabolical in nature. Jesus Christ told us that we could "speak" to these spiritual mountains. We can speak to them to move in our favor if we have no doubt in our heart that the things we say shall come to pass. In Mark 11:22-23 Jesus said to the disciples, *"Have faith in God. I tell you the truth, you can say to this mountain, 'May you be lifted up and thrown into the sea,' and it will happen. But you must really believe it will happen and have no doubt in your heart."*

In the above passage of Scripture, the Lord Jesus Christ tells us plainly that if we had faith in God we would be able to move any spiritual mountain in our favor for the purpose of advancing God's Kingdom here on earth. The original Hebrew translation of this verse literally means, "to have the faith of God". In order to operate in the God kind of faith there must be complete and harmonious agreement between what we confess with our mouth and what we believe in our heart. Anything short of this will short circuit the flow of God's power through our lives. Spiritual integrity in what we say and believe is an unavoidable necessity of operating in the God-kind of faith.

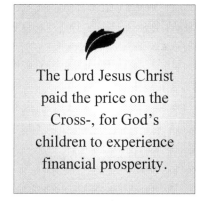

The Lord Jesus Christ paid the price on the Cross-, for God's children to experience financial prosperity.

All global currencies fall under the Mountain of Finance. In the global world of commerce, it is impossible for any nation to run its economy smoothly without subscribing to a widely accepted form of local currency. This local currency acts as legal tender or the medium of exchange for the flow of goods and services. This local currency is the accepted legal tender for satisfying all forms of financial obligations within that economy. It is impossible to separate the strength of a nation's economy from the strength of its local currency on the global market. It therefore follows that a nation's buying power correlates with the strength of its local currency and its federal reserves. The Mountain of Finance controls the flow of all global currencies, including major currencies such as the US dollar, British pound, Japanese Yen, and Eurodollar just to name a few.

The Flow of Investment Capital

The Mountain of Finance also controls the flow of investment capital for new business ventures: it determines the interest rates for borrowing and lending. This aspect of the Mountain of Finance goes all the way back to the time of Joseph, Jacob's eleventh son, after he became the prime minister of Egypt.

Then the seven years of famine began, just as Joseph had predicted. The famine also struck all the surrounding countries, but throughout Egypt there was plenty of food. Eventually, however, the famine spread throughout the land of Egypt as well. And when the people cried out to Pharaoh for food, he told them, "Go to Joseph, and do whatever he tells you." So with severe famine everywhere, Joseph opened up the storehouses and distributed grain to the Egyptians, for the famine was severe throughout the land of Egypt. And people from all around came to Egypt to buy grain from

Joseph because the famine was severe throughout the world.
Genesis 41:54-57

Without a shadow of doubt Joseph is truly the first bona-fide Kingdom finance minister. Many of present day regulations and practices in the Mountain of Finance (banking) were initiated by Joseph who was able to steward the economy of Egypt in one of the worst economic famines in Scripture. When we closely examine Joseph's tenure as the prime minister of Egypt we quickly begin to see the strong connection between the Mountain of Finance and the flow of investment capital for new business ventures. Since the Mountain of Finance controls much of the investment capital for new business ventures, you can understand why demonic powers have positioned themselves in this mountain. They want to resist and quarantine the flow of investment capital to God's people who are trying to build the Kingdom. The demonic principality, Babylon the Great, fights ferociously against the release of the necessary financing needed to finance gospel crusades and new Kingdom businesses and churches. How else would you explain why churches, who are among the biggest depositories, struggle to get funding from the same banking systems they help grow rich with new deposits every Monday morning?

(as it is written, "I have made you a father of many nations")
in the presence of Him whom he believed—God, who gives
life to the dead and calls those things which do not exist as
though they did; Romans 4:17 (NKJV)

Since the Mountain of Finance is a spiritual mountain or system it can be compelled by our faith-filled proclamations to align itself in a favorable position towards the Kingdom. The Bible calls this practice, "calling those things that are not as though they were." (Romans 4:17) We must not be afraid to use our God given spiritual authority to command the Mountain of Finance to release all the necessary financing needed to advance the Kingdom of God and fund our business career! Jesus told us that if we spoke to these mountains in faith, and have no doubt in our heart, "whatever we say shall come to pass!" We will see miraculous answers to our prayers as God moves these seven mountains in our favor.

TAXATION

Then Joseph said to the people, "Look, today I have bought you and your land for Pharaoh. I will provide you with seed so you can plant the fields. Then when you harvest it, one-fifth of your crop will belong to Pharaoh. You may keep the remaining four-fifths as seed for your fields and as food for you, your households, and your little ones." "You have saved our lives!" they exclaimed. "May it please you, my lord, to let us be Pharaoh's servants." Joseph then issued a decree still in effect in the land of Egypt, that Pharaoh should receive one-fifth of all the crops grown on his land. Genesis 47:23-25

The Mountain of Finance also controls the taxation of corporations and individuals alike. Joseph was the first government official to introduce the concept of taxing corporate and personal income to fund and drive the machinery of government. I know most people do not enjoy paying taxes to the government: I too am guilty as charged. The most hated government institution in the United States is the Internal Revenue Service, acronym IRS! I have yet to meet a person (believers included) in the United States who prays fervently for God to bless the IRS. In certain settings, it is almost scandalous to mention the IRS and yet one would have to admit that without the IRS many of the federal public services we take for granted would disappear or grind to a screeching halt. Many of us who live in the United States are defended by the greatest military in the whole world. But this would not be possible if it were not for the tax dollars of working Americans that finance the needs of our strong military.

As soon as the Israelite army saw him, they began to run away in fright. "Have you seen the giant?" the men asked. "He comes out each day to defy Israel. The king has offered a huge reward to anyone who kills him. He will give that man one of his daughters for a wife, and the man's entire family will be exempted from paying taxes!" 1 Samuel 17:24-25

Since taxation is part of the Mountain of Finance we can prophetically speak to this mountain to give us favorable tax settlements. After David killed Goliath, David and his entire family were released from paying taxes to the government by the king's decree. I mention this story to simply say, God is able to bring us into favorable circumstances where our taxes are either wiped out or lowered significantly.

> *The leaders of Israel summoned him, and Jeroboam and the whole assembly of Israel went to speak with Rehoboam. "Your father was a hard master," they said. "Lighten the harsh labor demands and heavy taxes that your father imposed on us. Then we will be your loyal subjects."* 1 Kings 12:3-4

Since the Mountain of Finance is a spiritual mountain-kingdom that is more often than not driven by the spirit of Babylon, it is not uncommon to see the rise of demonically engineered taxes that are designed to burden the people, stifle the marketplace, and slow the advancement of the Kingdom of God. Believers must use their God-given authority and declare, "We speak to the Mountain of Finance; we decree and declare that all demonically engineered taxes that are incubated in satanic wombs will not materialize in our state or country. All demonically engineered legislation designed to raise taxes in order to hinder the prosperity of God's children or delay the fulfillment of God's eternal plans and purposes, will ultimately fail!" As ambassadors of the Kingdom of God we must not be afraid to pray this type of governmental warfare prayer over the Mountain of Finance.

THE MAKING OF A KINGDOM FINANCE MINISTER

Joseph's life story provides us with a prophetic backdrop of how God prepares a Kingdom finance minister. Joseph's pride was dashed to pieces through the things he suffered so he could learn humility. There is no character trait more important for any Joseph of Arimathea than the trait of humility. Humility will keep you at the pinnacle of your mountain. God allowed Joseph's brothers to betray him so he could learn how to lean on God. A beautiful and lustful woman in the form of Potiphar's wife tried to seduce him, so he could rise above the seductive power of sexual sin. Men and

Joseph, was the first government official to introduce the concept of taxing corporate and personal income.

women who are called to be Josephs of Arimathea must know that sexual sin will quickly destroy their calling. Joseph was also tested in money management while he was working for Potiphar. Potiphar left everything he owned under Joseph's care. It could have been so easy for Joseph to help himself to his master's money.

Joseph was also tested in how he managed people when he went to prison. To say that prisoners are not always the easiest people to get along with may well be an understatement. He was tested in how he managed political power when he became Egypt's prime minister. He did not exact revenge on Potiphar or his lying wife even

There is no character trait more important for any Joseph of Arimathea than the trait of humility.

though he could have. He was tested in his ability to walk in forgiveness when his brothers who had sold him into slavery arrived at his doorstep asking for help. Finally, Joseph was tested in how he managed the corporate destiny when he chose to sustain his brothers, together with their families, after his father Jacob died. Many true Joseph of Arimathea can attest to the fact that God also tested them before He bestowed great wealth on their shoulders.

THE MOUNTAIN OF FAMILY

A father of the fatherless, a defender of widows, is God in His holy habitation. God sets the solitary in families; Psalms 68:5-6

The Mountain of Family is one of the most relational of the Seven Mountains of Culture. The Mountain of Family controls the relationship between husband and wives, fathers and sons, and between mothers and daughters. In the second chapter of Genesis, God established, the Mountain of Family on the foundation of the institution of marriage between male and female. Any attempt to redefine marriage as other than being the sexual union of a man and a woman will only destroy the spiritual foundation of the Mountain of Family.

Therefore, a man shall leave his father and mother and be joined to his wife, and they shall become one flesh. And they were both naked, the man and his wife, and were not ashamed. Genesis 2:24-25

The Mountain of Family controls the moral and core values of any person born of a woman here on earth. This would explain why the devil fights so hard to destroy the Mountain of Family. When people come from families with strong moral and core values they are not easily tempted to follow the devil. Needless to say, persons who come from families with weak moral and core values are the playing ground of demonic spirits. Whatever moral and core values a person learns from the Mountain of Family will determine his or her conduct in the other six mountain-kingdoms. This is why the Mountain of Family is so important.

The custodians of the Mountain of Family are fathers and mothers. God gave parents the spiritual authority to train and discipline their children. Fathers and mothers are very important players in the Mountain of Family. It has been reported that children who grow up in single parent homes are more likely to break the law and end up in jail. Most of the children from single parent homes have serious emotional attachment disorders. Spiritual fathering and mothering is God's method for correcting whatever has been broken in the Mountain of Family. Spiritual fathering and mothering is when God uses a man or woman of God to take on a parenting role in the life of a believer. The Mountain of Family is the training ground for the leaders, husbands and wives of tomorrow! Please remember that your son is the future husband of someone else's daughter and your daughter is the future wife of someone else's son. So how are you raising them?

Train up a child in the way he should go, And when he is old he will not depart from it. Proverbs 22:6

No other mountain reveals the desire of God to have a spiritual family of His own like the Mountain of Family. God has always wanted to have a family (Ephesians 3:15). The first shedding of human blood in the Bible took place in the Mountain of Family, showing us that Satan's primary assignment is to destroy the Mountain of Family. Satan loves to incite strife and violence in family relationships, even to the point of shedding blood. It has been reported that most homicides take place within the Mountain of Family (Genesis 4:1-12). Most homicide detectives focus on interviewing family members before they look elsewhere. Nothing shatters the foundation of family like the spirit of divorce, because the bedrock of the Mountain of Family is the institution of marriage between husband and wife. Spirits of strife, violence and adultery are Satan's favorite weapons against those who are trying to climb the Mountain of Family. Jesus gave a very stern warning of the impending judgment that will befall those who destroy the Mountain of Family (Matthew 19:6).

The Mountain of Family is the first spiritual and natural covering God gives to children of destiny before giving them a pastor. The devil tried to destroy Jesus when He was just a baby but God protected Him within the Mountain of Family when He spoke to his father Joseph to take the family to Egypt (Matthew 2:13-15). Satan's primary entrance into the Mountain of Family is through generational curses. A generational curse is a curse that is attached to the genes (DNA) a person received from his or her ancestors that causes them to repeat unacceptable behaviors or flawed traits of their ancestors. Knowing how to break generational curses and how to cast out demons will prove very helpful to those who want to climb to the top of the Mountain of Family and build strong families. There are people whose primary assignment in the Kingdom is dealing with family issues to bring the Mountain of Family under God's influence. Dr. James Dobson's "Focus on the Family" and Jim Evans' "Marriage Today" are primary examples of ministries dedicated to fighting demons and attitudes which destroy families. God will reward those who dedicate their life and ministry to warring for the preservation of the sanctity of family life.

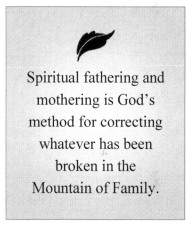

Spiritual fathering and mothering is God's method for correcting whatever has been broken in the Mountain of Family.

THE MOUNTAIN OF
MEDIA, ARTS & ENTERTAINMENT

One of the most influential of the seven mountains is the Mountain of Media, Arts & Entertainment. Some Bible teachers separate this mountain into two mountains, the Mountain of Media and the Mountain of Arts & Entertainment but I have always combined them to make room for the Mountain of Finance. The Mountain of Media, Arts & Entertainment controls what is happening in the world of television, movies, the arts, as well as the entertainment industry. Sports and sporting events such as the World Cup and the Olympics are under this mountain. If you live in the United States, all you have to do is turn on the television and you will be bombarded by the power of the media. The United States is famous for our endless 24-hour news cycles.

The Mountain of Media, Arts & Entertainment also controls the flow of public opinion through television, newspapers and talk radio. No politician can win the presidency without passing through this very strategic mountain-kingdom. If you are called to this mountain it is critical that you remain aware of your role in creating public opinion and even impacting the moral climate. One has only to look at television programming to understand how this mountain forms and impacts the morals of our children. According to a study by the University of Michigan, children ages 2-5 spend 32 hours a week watching television[7] yet a survey by Virgin Holidays and Orlando Resorts found that parents only spend 36 minutes a day (that equates to 3.5 hours a week) with their children[8] so it is easy to see who has greater influence in determining opinions and attitudes in our youth. When the Mountain of Media, Arts & Entertainment is brought under the governing influence of the Kingdom of God it not only has the power to reach multiplied millions of people with the Gospel of Jesus Christ it has the power to strengthen families. Churches or businesses that do not have a deep respect for the Mountain of Media, Arts & Entertainment can never become governing influences in the city.

The Mountain of Media, Arts & Entertainment has spawned some of the most well-known celebrities, because of the global influence of the arts and entertainment industry on the global populace. There is literally no nation on earth that has not been influenced by movies coming out of Hollywood, the entertainment capital of the world. People on our planet know the names Denzel Washington, Meryl Streep, Matt Damon, Michael Jordan, Lebron James or Serena Williams more than they know the name of the Queen of England. This is because most people's hobbies usually revolve around the arts and entertainment. Consequentially they are actively involved in the world of sports and entertainment. Kingdom entrepreneurs, especially those called specifically to this mountain, must know how to work within this mountain in order to advance their business interests, strengthen families and change the moral fabric of their nation.

THE MOUNTAIN OF RELIGION

And I also say to you that you are Peter, and on this rock I will build My church, and the gates of Hades shall not prevail against it. Matthew 16:18

The Mountain of Religion is by far the most important of the Seven Mountains of Culture because it controls the spiritual destinies of all the people on the earth. It holds the key to the salvation or damnation of men's eternal souls. There is absolutely nothing more precious and priceless than the salvation of the soul. Man's soul and spirit live forever, long after the body is dead. This explains man's obsession with the question of immortality. Jesus said it this way, *"What shall it profit a man to gain the whole world and lose his soul?"* (Mark 8:36) Man's search for immortality is the reason the world we live in is full of many religions that all claim to answer man's deepest quest.

Churches or businesses that do not have a deep respect for the Mountain of Media, Arts & Entertainment can never become governing churches or businesses in the City.

The spiritual power of the Mountain of Religion is rooted in its attempt to answer five of mankind's most important questions, namely:

- Where did I come from?

- Why am I here?
- What is my purpose?
- How should I live my life?
- Where am I going when I die?

Born again believers are key players in the Mountain of Religion because we know the answers to these questions with absolute certainty. Jesus' birth, life, suffering, death, and resurrection answered all the above questions. The Mountain of Religion controls every form of religion or expression of faith known to mankind. World religions such as Catholicism, Hinduism, Buddhism, Islam, Judaism and even Christianity all fall under the Mountain of Religion. The Roman Catholic Church has established itself as the most powerful institutional churches within the Mountain of Religion

The primary focus of the Mountain of Religion is the worship of a deity, followed by adherence to a specified religious code of conduct and obedience to the presiding priesthood of the deity. The Mountain of Religion has the power to open the portals of heaven for lost souls as well as shut down the gates of hell (Matthew 16:17-19). This mountain also has the power to close the portals of heaven to lost souls and open the gates of hell whenever the Devil seizes control of this mountain, as he does in false religions that don't believe Jesus Christ is the only way to God (Matthew 23:13-16).

The corridors of human history and the recent resurgence of religious Jihad have shown us that many people will gladly die for their religion even before dying for their country. Such is the power of the Mountain of Religion over the souls of men. This would also explain why the devil fights very hard to control the Mountain of Religion. To effectively shift and align this mountain under the influence of the Kingdom of God, the church must be built on the foundation of apostles and prophets with Christ Jesus as the Chief Cornerstone (Ephesians 2:20). In Ephesus for instance, after two years of Paul's apostolic ministry the Mountain of Religion shifted radically towards the Kingdom of God. There was a sweeping revival such that many people in Ephesus no longer went to the temple of Diana the great goddess of the Ephesians to worship. They even stopped buying articles related to the worship of Diana (Acts 19:23-28).

Jesus said it this way, "What shall it profit a man to gain the whole world and lose his soul?"

The quickest way to bring the Mountain of Religion under the spiritual control of demons is to move it away from its apostolic and prophetic foundations and replace them with a legalistic and political spirit. For instance, Jesus called the Pharisees and Sadducees sons of the devil even though they were the leaders of the church in Jerusalem. This is because they were very legalistic and political in their approach to matters of faith. They had single handedly managed to bring the Mountain of Religion into the dark ages (John 8:44-50). I strongly advise Kingdom entrepreneurs who are called to be a Joseph of Arimathea to be firmly planted in a Bible believing and Christ-centered church. It's so easy for wealthy people to stay busy and stop faithfully attending church. I am convinced that every Joseph of Arimathea needs to be under a functional spiritual covering of a man or woman God that they respect.

THE MOUNTAIN OF BUSINESS

It is the glory of God to conceal a matter, but the glory of kings is to search out a matter. Proverbs 25:2 NAS

...money is the answer for everything. Eccl 10:19, NIV

But remember the LORD your God, for it is he who gives you the ability to produce wealth, and so confirms his covenant, which he swore to your ancestors, as it is today. Deuteronomy 8:18, NIV

Dictionary.com defines business as, "a person, partnership, or corporation engaged in commerce, manufacturing, or a service; profit seeking enterprise or concern." Dr. Gordon Bradshaw, in his book I See Thrones, defines business this way:

"A business, also known as an enterprise or firm, is an organization involved in the trade of goods, services or both, to consumers. Businesses are prevalent in capitalist economies, where most of them are privately owned and provide goods and services to customers in exchange for other goods, services or money (Wikipedia). Business, in some shape, form or fashion, takes place in every area of the Earth that's inhabited by mankind. It too, affects every other mountain of culture in terms of how the goods and services that are associated with each mountain are made available to the public. It is essential for the survival and upward mobility of cultures and societies on this planet. Higher Education systems have been established to teach the trade of business, with schools such as Harvard University, Stanford University, the London School of Economics, Yale University, Cambridge University, the University of Chicago, University of Pennsylvania, Dartmouth College, the Kellogg School of Business and numerous others, leading the way. Business is so important to the health of this planet that many nations form governmental regulatory groups to oversee transactions to ensure fairness and adherence to laws of trade and commerce." [9]

It can easily be said that "business makes the world go round" because everything we eat, wear, drive, and possess was created by a business, transported by a business, sold by a business and once purchased, the maintenance is handled by a business. There is no part of our life that is not touched by business and that includes the other six mountains. That is why it is so critical that all those engaged in the Joseph of Arimathea calling fully understand the impact of the Mountain of Business as well as the necessity of establishing relationships and interacting with the other mountains.

Even though I function primarily as an apostle to the nations from the Mountain of Religion I have always been fascinated by business. The Mountain of Business is truly a critical mountain-kingdom because it is the largest single employer of the people on this planet, followed by the Mountain of Law and Government. When this mountain-kingdom sneezes it sends shivers in the spine of any economy. When the Mountain of Business struggles to make profit massive layoffs of people always occurs. What I love the most about the Mountain of Business is that it is responsible for the large fortunes many private citizens own. This is because this mountain, above all others, is driven by the desire to make a profit. I am convinced that many of the end-time Joseph of Arimathea's are coming from the Mountain of Business. The Holy Spirit is going to show them how to do business supernaturally.

> I am convinced that every Joseph of Arimathea needs to be under a functional "spiritual covering" of a man or woman God that they respect.

THE MOUNTAIN OF EDUCATION

Then the king ordered Ashpenaz, the chief of his officials, to bring in some of the sons of Israel, including some of the royal family and of the nobles, youths in whom was no defect, who were good-looking, showing intelligence in every branch of wisdom, endowed with understanding and discerning knowledge, and who had ability for serving in the king's court; and he ordered him to teach them the literature and language of the Chaldeans. Daniel 1:3-4, NAS

God gave these four young men an unusual aptitude for understanding every aspect of literature and wisdom. And God gave Daniel the special ability to interpret the meanings of visions and dreams. When the training period ordered by the king was completed, the chief of staff brought all the young men to King Nebuchadnezzar. The king talked with them, and no one impressed him as much as Daniel, Hananiah, Mishael and Azariah; so, they entered the royal service. Whenever the king consulted them in any matter requiring wisdom and balanced judgment he found them "ten times more capable than any of the magicians and enchanters in his entire kingdom." (Daniel 1:17-20, NLT)

In Dr. Gordon Bradshaw's book, I See Thrones, he states: "Education is defined as: "The action or process of educating or being educated; a field of study dealing with methods of teaching and learning." (Webster's New Explorer Dictionary and Thesaurus). The
168

Education Mountain relates to the professionally structured system of gathering and disseminating information to create an environment for learning, processing and acting upon what we've learned. What we learn as a human race is very important because it reflects upon how we conduct ourselves as citizens, how we contribute to the preservation of life, how we treat our resources and each other, and how we become productive contributors to society. How we learn is as important as what we learn.

God is raising kings in this mountain who know how to stimulate the learning experience and how to pass on more information than we've ever done before. These are people who have new and creative ways of helping others become all that they can be through diversified teaching methods. Each one of the seven mountains have an educational process that empowers the people who function in these mountains, making the quality of education of the highest importance. The advancement of the best practices in any field or industry relies a great deal on how well its participants are educated."[10]

The Mountain of Education has far reaching impact in our culture because it forms the perspectives, shapes the ideologies, and controls the minds of the people of today and the leaders of tomorrow. This mountain influences the educational process of each of the other seven mountains. If you want to be a successful businessperson, you will need to go through this mountain to earn your MBA, before launching your business career. If you want to be a movie producer or screenplay writer, you will still have to pass through this mountain. If you want to become a medical doctor so you can open your own practice, you still have to go through the Mountain of Education. We can go through several scenarios and the conclusion will be the same: we all must pass through the Mountain of Education. This is why some of the people that the Holy Spirit is raising in the office of Joseph of Arimathea in the Body of Christ will be assigned to the Mountain of Education. Those who are involved in the private sector of education will make tremendous fortunes from this highly influential mountain.

A PRIEST
ON HIS THRONE

TOOLS FOR WEALTH CREATION

ONE OF THE CRITICAL ISSUES of the last days is how the global church can come into its God-given financial inheritance. One of the mountains that must come into total subjection to allow the Body of Christ worldwide to express its kingly and priestly ministry in its totality is the Mountain of Finance. This mountain must bow to the authority of Christ and His Kingdom through His universal body, the Church.

A feast is made for laughter, and wine makes merry; But money answers everything. Ecclesiastes 10:19

The writer of the book of Ecclesiastes tells us that money is the answer to all things! Money is the answer to so many things that we need within the realms of men. Money (currency) is the medium of exchange for all goods and services within this earthly realm of reality. If I want to fly to Asia to preach the gospel of Jesus Christ, I will need money to buy air tickets, book hotels, and pay for the costs of the crusade. For people who are troubled by the plight of child sex-slaves, rescuing these innocent souls from the cartels will require a large sum of money. It's no wonder there are four times more scriptures in the Bible relating to money than there are on prayer. I am glad that the Bible is not silent on this important subject, which is a critical factor in advancing the Gospel of the Kingdom.

For several decades, the Church has been bombarded by messages from well-meaning televangelists who promised it the supernatural wealth transfer which, for the most part, has not materialized in the life of many ardent followers of Christ. This proverbial disconnect between the promise, the vision, and the provision has caused many Christ followers and ministries to come into a place of total frustration and discouragement. For the longest, I sought the Holy Spirit as to why the Church was failing to enter into the promised supernatural transfer of wealth from the hands of the wicked to the just.

A good man leaves an inheritance to his children's children,
But the wealth of the sinner is stored up for the righteous.
Proverbs 13:22

A PRIEST WITH A THRONE

Now of the things which we have spoken this is the sum: We have such a high priest, who is set on the right hand of the throne of the Majesty in the heavens; Hebrews 8:1

Yes, [you are building a temple of the Lord, but] it is He Who shall build the [true] temple of the Lord, and He shall bear the honor and glory [as of the only begotten of the Father] and shall sit and rule upon His throne. And He shall be a Priest upon His throne, and the counsel of peace shall be between the two [offices—Priest and King]. Zechariah 6:13, (Amplified)

The above passage is part of the prophetic vision that God gave to the Prophet Zechariah concerning the restoration of the Melchizedek Priesthood in the person of Jesus and the coming supernatural wealth transfer through the merging of the kingly and priestly graces of the Lord Jesus Christ. What is most interesting about the prophecy of the Prophet Zechariah is that in the prophecy the prophet mentions a unique characteristic of this new priesthood that was not readily available to the Old Testament Levitical priesthood. This unique characteristic would become the distinguishing factor between the

The priestly ministry of the man called the "Branch" (Jesus) would combine the functions of a king to that of a priest.

two priestly orders making one higher than the other by the same unique characteristic. This unique characteristic was contained and captured in the elaborate royal crown and the makeshift throne that were both created by the gold-and-silver that came from Jewish captives from Babylon. Crowns and thrones are unique to kingdoms. They infer dominion and royalty. Consequently, the priesthood of a priest who wears a crown and sits on a throne is of a higher order than the Levitical priest who lacked accruements

THE DYNAMICS OF CROWNS AND THRONES

The moment Prophet Zechariah coroneted Joshua (Yeshua in Hebrew) in Zechariah 6 by laying the royal crown on his head, Joshua was completely transformed. His priestly ministry changed radically through the single act of coronation. He went from being a mere priest under the Levitical priesthood and became a king-priest, after the Order of Melchizedek (Genesis 14:18).

The prophet was then instructed by God to sit Joshua onto a makeshift throne after the coronation. As soon as Joshua, who was wearing the crown on his head, sat on the makeshift throne, the prophet made a startling announcement: that the priestly ministry of the man called the "Branch" (Jesus) would combine the functions of a king to that of a priest. In other words, the coming king will also be a priest. This is a powerful and dazzling combination. Just remember that this entire prophetic act and demonstration of the coming priesthood of Jesus Christ was happening in front of all the Levitical

174

priests of that era. Through the wisdom of God, the Levites were being told that they would soon be replaced by a higher and more powerful priestly order that will combine the functions of a king to that of a priest. The only God-ordained priesthood in the entire Bible that merges the kingly and priestly anointing under one tent is the "Order of Melchizedek" (Genesis 14:18).

A MAN LIKE NO OTHER

Now after Jesus was born in Bethlehem of Judea in the days of Herod the king, behold, wise men from the East came to Jerusalem, saying, "Where is He who has been born King of the Jews? For we have seen His star in the East and have come to worship Him." ... And when they had come into the house, they saw the young Child with Mary His mother, and fell down and worshiped Him. And when they had opened their treasures, they presented gifts to Him: gold, frankincense, and myrrh. Matthew 2:1-2, 11

My dear friends, there is no man in human history that has ever been able to fulfill this prophetic picture from the book of Zechariah like the Lord Jesus Christ. From the time when Jesus Christ was born in the manger, magi from the East entered Jerusalem to come and worship the newly born King (Matthew 2). Guided by the rise of a powerful Eastern star, the magi found their way to the baby in swaddling clothes. They came bearing gifts worthy of a great king. God Almighty in His eternal genius used the magi from the East to coronate the King of the universe when He entered into His own world through the virgin birth.

The prophet Zechariah declares that the man whose name is the "Branch" shall be a priest on His throne. As a priest on His throne he would rule the nations. Since the priest has a throne in this prophetic analogy it follows that the priest is also a king over a kingdom. Only kingdoms have thrones. Since the high priest in this prophetic analogy is a king with a kingdom it follows that kingdom principles and laws of governance drive the machinery of his priestly order.

What is truly exciting here is that the only priestly order in scripture that allows a king to be a priest is the Order of Melchizedek. Through this one prophetic act, the Prophet Zechariah was foreshadowing the return of the Melchizedek priesthood to a greater body of believers than the Levitical priesthood would allow. Under the Levitical priesthood only male members of the tribe of Levi could be admitted into the priesthood. Every other believer in Israel was excluded from the priesthood. Fortunately for us, God was about to change the rules of the game. An ancient and more powerful priestly order was coming to our planet that would include a greater body of believers into the priesthood. This ancient priestly order was a priesthood that would integrate the activities of Kingdom citizens in the marketplace and in the temple, seamlessly!

SUPERNATURAL WEALTH TRANSFER

*A good man leaveth an inheritance to his children's children:
and the wealth of the sinner is laid up for the just.* Proverbs
13:22

What is of critical importance here is to notice that the
emergence of this new priesthood would involve the plundering of
all the gold and silver of the Babylonian financial system by citizens
of the Kingdom of God. The angel who spoke to the prophet
Zechariah told him that the four companies of high-ranking cherubim
angels (Zechariah 6:1-9) were given a high-level Kingdom
assignment to plunder the nation of its supply of gold and silver and
use it to create royal crowns to coronate the children of the Kingdom.
Notice here that the long anticipated supernatural wealth transfer is
intricately connected to the coronation of the children of the
Kingdom as kings and priests unto God (Revelation 1:6). Without
this understanding, the Church (Body of Christ) will remain stationed
outside the golden gates of its God-given spiritual inheritance.

For the most part, many churches function under a Levitical
system of worship and ministry. This Levitical mindset that
overemphasizes the importance of the temple (at the expense of the
church actively engaging the marketplace), thwarts the process of the
much needed transition from a local priestly-based church to a
broader based kingly and priestly ministry. Nevertheless, this
transition must take place before the Body of Christ can experience
the much-awaited supernatural transfer of wealth. Without this divine

177

coronation of the saints as kings and priests under the Order of Melchizedek this proverbial promise will continue to elude the church's grip.

In the institutional church, the majority of the members of the Body of Christ have been relegated to being mere members of the laity forever trapped in an ever-shrinking middle class. This massive company of potential kings and priests are expected every Sunday to warm the pews of the church while the favored few perform for them. This technology of ministry, which does not value the marketplace mantles of this massive company of Kingdom citizens, does not lend itself to the release of the end-time supernatural transfer of wealth.

The only priestly order in Scripture that allows a king to be a priest is the Order of Melchizedek.

A BLOOD BOUGHT CORONATION!

And from Jesus Christ, who is the faithful witness, and the first begotten of the dead, and the prince of the kings of the earth. Unto him that loved us, and washed us from our sins in his own blood, And hath made us kings and priests unto God and his Father; to him be glory and dominion for ever and ever. Amen. Revelation 1:5-6

Many Christians around the world reverence the shed blood of Jesus Christ, as well they should. But for the most part what His shed blood has purchased for the new creation is relegated to the mere cleansing from sin. Even though cleansing from sin is a vital part of the redeeming power of the blood of Jesus Christ, it's not the ultimate objective as to why the blood of Jesus Christ was shed. Cleansing from sin through the blood of Jesus Christ was merely a means to an end. The end that God sought in having His Precious Son shed His blood for us, was to restore all mankind to the position of stature in the economy of the Kingdom that Adam and Eve forfeited in the Garden of Eden. It's the sin consciousness of the Church that causes believers to fail to enter all that the shed blood purchased for the new creation.

Recently, a friend of mine, Dr. Jesse Bielby, shared a scripture that I have read many times before but had failed to see its obvious connection to the Melchizedek Priesthood of Jesus Christ. The passage of scripture was Revelation 1:5-6: *"And from Jesus Christ, who is the faithful witness, and the first begotten of the dead, and the prince of the kings of the earth. Unto him that loved us, and washed us from our sins in his own blood, And hath made us kings and priests unto God and his Father; to him be glory and dominion for ever and ever. Amen."* This passage makes a staggering connection between the shed blood of Jesus Christ and our ability as children of God to function in the earth as kings and priests. It is clear from this passage that the primary reason why the blood of Jesus

Christ was shed was to cleanse us from sin, so that we can be made kings and priests unto God!

Think of this: the blood of Christ was shed to make it possible for sinners who are made righteous to instantly become a kingdom of kings and priests unto God. Stated in another way, the shed blood of Jesus Christ PAID for our supernatural coronation as kings and priests unto God in the earth realm. His shed blood restored the royal priesthood of the royal family of God! This is why I continue to insist that the promised supernatural transfer of wealth from the wicked to the righteous will never take place in its fullness until the Church enters into an accurate understanding of the Melchizedek Priesthood of Jesus Christ. All Kingdom entrepreneurs who desire to be used by God must keep this in mind.

HEADS CROWNED WITH GOLD AND SILVER

Accept donations and offerings from these [as representatives of the] exiles, from Heldai, from Tobijah, and from Jedaiah, who have come from Babylon; and come the same day and go to the house of Josiah the son of Zephaniah. Yes, take from them silver and gold, and make crowns and set [one] upon the head of Joshua the son of Jehozadak, the high priest. Zechariah 6:10-11, (Amplified)

In the sixth chapter of the book of Zechariah, the angel of the Lord tells the prophet that the four companies of high-ranking cherubim from the throne of God were on an assignment to crown the children of the Kingdom with crowns made of gold and silver that were taken from the world's Babylonian financial system. My dear friend these high-ranking angelic beings are still patrolling the earth today with an assignment to plunder the nations of their supply of gold and silver for the purpose of crowning the saints. This coronation is the crowning of the children of God, who are being made into kings and priests unto God within the earth realm.

The long anticipated supernatural wealth transfer is intricately connected to the coronation of the children of the kingdom as kings and priests unto God (Revelation 1:6).

Here is a truth that is of critical importance: this divine crowning of the children of the Kingdom will not take place until the Church understands and enters into the Order of Melchizedek. The Order of Melchizedek is the only divinely inspired priesthood in the Bible that allows both the kingly and priestly mantles to function together in one body seamlessly. The Melchizedek who intercepted Abram in the Valley of the Kings in Genesis 14 was a king-priest.

CROWNS = WEALTH GENERATING IDEAS

What is also interesting to note here is that the royal crowns that the Melchizedek priesthood of Jesus Christ is bestowing upon the saints, are made of gold and silver. It does not take a rocket scientist to figure out that gold and silver are two of the most important precious metals on the global market today. While the buying power of the US dollar and other FIAT currencies continue to decline because of massive national deficits and rising inflation, gold and silver are at an all-time high in value. Those who are fortunate enough to have these two metals in their investment portfolios are smiling their way to the bank.

Prophetically speaking, a crown of gold and silver around our heads implies that God is going to crown His royal priesthood on earth with wealth generating ideas. Dr. Myles Munroe stated that there is nothing more powerful than an idea. Ideas rule and control the world. I am convinced that the best technological, medical, and scientific breakthroughs have not yet been discovered. Those whom God will trust with these end-time cutting edge breakthroughs are going to become multi-billionaires, almost overnight. Some of the best sales and marketing ideas have not yet been harvested. The children of the Kingdom who will be given these innovative ideas will become major economic powerbrokers. Some of the best books and movies have not yet been written and those who the Holy Spirit will entrust with these assets will become extremely rich. Get ready for unprecedented wealth in the Body of Christ! The wealth of the wicked will be transferred to the righteous through these Holy Spirit inspired, inventions, breakthroughs, and business ideas. Glory to God Most High!!!

THRONES = SEATS OF POWER AND INFLUENCE

And I saw thrones, and they sat on them, and judgment was committed to them. Then I saw the souls of those who had been beheaded for their witness to Jesus and for the word of God, who had not worshiped the beast or his image, and had not received his mark on their foreheads or on their hands. And they lived and reigned with Christ for a thousand years.
Revelation 20:4

Thrones are kingdom concepts; they belong exclusively to the realm of kingdoms. In kingdoms, thrones are the highest seats of authority. They represent stature, ruler-ship, authority and influence. In Zechariah's prophetic act on behalf of Joshua (Zechariah 6:9-15) God instructed him to make a makeshift throne for Joshua, a Levitical priest, to sit on. After I saw this, the Holy Spirit showed me that the second tool God was going to use to manifest the supernatural transfer of wealth is the "Technology of Thrones!" In their simplest form, thrones are special seats of influence! "Son, I am going to give My people favor to occupy special seats of influence at the table of men and women with creative wealth generating ideas." Supernatural excitement flooded my spirit as I realized the practical ramifications of this revelation.

Case in point: Facebook was an idea born in the mind of Mark Zuckerberg before it became the massive multi-billion-dollar company it is today. Any high achiever who has ever given birth to a marketable idea, knows that conceiving the idea is one thing but

183

planting the idea in the ground and then taking it to marketplace requires a team. These team members become the guardians of the idea and the person who carries the idea until it becomes a product that can be sold to the masses. The team that guards and stewards the founder's idea usually become board or founding members.

Facebook was no different in its inception. Mark Zuckerberg's Facebook idea was surrounded by a team consisting of Eduardo Saverin, Andrew McCollum, Dustin Moskovitz, and Chris Hughes, fellow college students at Harvard University. When Facebook became a publicly traded company on the New York Stock Exchange, Mark Zuckerberg was not the only one who became a multi-millionaire overnight: his close associates who had special seats of influence, i.e., thrones in the Facebook corporate structure, also became multi-millionaires. We are about to experience the greatest supernatural transfer of wealth in the Body of Christ, since the world began because many Kingdom citizens are about to occupy thrones or seats of influence at the tables of men and women with incredible wealth generating ideas. Joseph in the Old Testament became a very rich and influential man in Egypt because Pharaoh gave him a very

A crown of gold and silver around our heads implies that God is going to crown His royal priesthood on earth with wealth generating ideas.

special seat of influence in his kingdom (Genesis 41:39-41). It is your time to prosper!

THE COUNSEL OF PEACE BETWEEN THE TWO OFFICES!

One of the casualties of the church's Levitical mindset is this sad and unnecessary division between the temple and the marketplace. This unfortunate divide between the Church and the marketplace lies at the root of the rapid moral decline of the United States of America and many other nations. The voices of secularism have trumpeted the separation of the church and the state, even though the founding fathers of the United States were men of faith in both private and public life. When you remove faith from public life there will be consequences because faith tends to speak to both individual and corporate morality. History books from the 1700s and 1800s on the United States clearly demonstrate that the founding fathers brought their private faith to their public service. No session of Congress ever started without offering prayer to acknowledge Divine providence, in the affairs of the United States government. Regrettably, in today's culture of misguided political correctness, it is taboo to bring matters of faith into public life. Consequently, there has been a deep and growing divide between the activities of the temple and that of the marketplace. This divide in American political life has actually become very hostile.

Sadly, most churches have accepted this sad state of affairs as the norm, because of bad theology that causes the Church to become an end in itself. In order to transform the culture we live in with the gospel of the Kingdom, the church must enter into the marketplace. The message and ministry of the Church can no longer be quarantined within the four walls of our church buildings. Thank God, through the emergence of the Melchizedek priesthood of Jesus Christ, the Holy Spirit is going to heal the division between the Church and the marketplace.

As the Church enters into an accurate understanding of the Melchizedek priesthood of Jesus Christ, which is a kingly and priestly ministry, the divide between church and state will collapse. The prophet Zechariah declares in Zechariah 6:13 that the priestly ministry of the Messiah (Jesus) shall bring the counsel of peace between the two offices of priest and king. The office of the priest allows the Body of Christ to function effectively in temple ministry, while the kingly office allows the Body of Christ to function effectively in marketplace ministry. It is clear that it has always been God's desire for these two offices, king and priest, to function in divine harmony. As the Church enters into the Order of Melchizedek the tension between the church and marketplace will come to an end. The Order of Melchizedek will bring about the counsel of peace between the two offices of priest and king. As the counsel of peace between the offices of king and priest is restored, the Church will become the greatest change agent in the affairs of nations. This kind of thinking will cause the Church to become a fertile breeding ground for many Josephs of Arimathea who will use their wealth and political influence to rescue the Body of Christ from being destroyed by forces opposed to the cause of Christ.

WHAT SHALL
IT PROFIT A MAN?

For what will it profit a man if he gains the whole world, and
loses his own soul? Mark 8:36

IN CONCLUSION, I want the rich or super-wealthy members of the Body of Christ and all those aspiring to the office of Joseph of Arimathea to ask themselves the most consequential question of all. It's a question that rings true through the ages. It's one of the greatest questions that Jesus Christ ever asked during His earthly pilgrimage. "What will it profit a man if he gains the whole world, and loses his own soul?" What a sobering question. I believe that hell is full of the world's super-wealthy who never took the time while they were alive to answer Jesus' question. I am sure most of the world's wealthy who ended up in hell after their short existence here on earth, would welcome the chance for a do-over. I am reminded of the story of the rich man and Lazarus.

THE RICH MAN AND LAZARUS

There was a certain rich man who was clothed in purple and fine linen and fared sumptuously every day. But there was a certain beggar named Lazarus, full of sores, who was laid at his gate, desiring to be fed with the crumbs which fell[d] from the rich man's table. Moreover the dogs came and licked his sores. So it was that the beggar died, and was carried by the angels to Abraham's bosom. The rich man also died and was buried. And being in torments in Hades, he lifted up his eyes and saw Abraham afar off, and Lazarus in his bosom. "Then he cried and said, 'Father Abraham, have mercy on me, and send Lazarus that he may dip the tip of his finger in water and cool my tongue; for I am tormented in this flame.' But Abraham said, 'Son, remember that in your lifetime you received your good things, and likewise Lazarus evil things; but now he is comforted and you are tormented. And besides all this, between us and you there is a great gulf fixed, so that those who want to pass from here to you cannot, nor can those from there pass to us.' "Then he said, 'I beg you therefore, father, that you would send him to my father's house, for I have five brothers, that he may testify to them, lest they also come to this place of torment.' Abraham said to him, 'They have Moses and the prophets; let them hear them.' And he said, 'No, father Abraham; but if one goes to them from the dead, they will repent.' But he said to him, 'If they do not hear

Moses and the prophets, neither will they be persuaded though one rise from the dead.'" Luke 16:19-31

The story of the rich man and Lazarus is truly a story that those who are rich and wealthy in the Body of Christ and in the world, cannot afford to ignore. What is interesting about the story is that Jesus did not tell it as a parable. He told it as a true story. In this instance he was not trying to teach through metaphor; He was recounting an actual event that took place.

The reason the Bible does not give us the name of the rich man is because the principal behind the story is more important than the individual. In other words, the story of the rich man and Lazarus has profound present, future, and eternal implications. As the story goes, Lazarus whose name means, "god is my help", was a beggar at the gates of the rich man's house. It would seem the rich man was so busy in acquiring more wealth that he never noticed the poor beggar at the gates to his mansion. According to the story, Lazarus died first and because he was a believer in the Lord the angels took him to Abraham's bosom in paradise. In the course of time the rich man also died. But instead of going to paradise he went straight to hell, where he was tormented in unquenchable flames.

Looking across the divide between paradise and hell he saw and recognized Lazarus in Abraham's bosom. He cried out to father Abraham and begged him to send Lazarus with a cup of water. Unfortunately, his request was not granted. But it is Abraham's diagnosis of his condition of torment that put chills of fear in my spine, the first time I read this passage of scripture. Abraham says to him, "Son, remember that in your lifetime you received your good things, and likewise Lazarus evil things; but now he is comforted and you are tormented." (Luke 16:25) Abraham's statement was not an indictment of this man's wealth while he was on earth, for Abraham had also been a very rich man when he was on earth. It was an indictment of his godless lifestyle while he was on earth. He had made the same mistake many wealthy people make; he had failed to answer Jesus's question – "What shall it profit a man to gain the whole world and yet lose his own soul?"

TRUE PROSPERITY

Beloved, I pray that you may prosper in all things and be in health, just as your soul prospers.

I have already established in Chapter Two of this book that the Lord wants His people to prosper in financial matters. God does not have a problem with his children being wealthy. This is an established biblical fact. However, the manner in which we prosper is very important to God. One of my favorite scriptures in the whole Bible is 3 John 2 which tells me how to prosper financially without losing my soul. This powerful scripture has three components that collectively describe the order of prosperity that God has established in His word. *"I pray that you may prosper in all things be in health as your soul prospers."* It is clear the soul prospering in righteousness

192

is a precursor to the following: Prospering in all things (this also includes prosperity in financial matters) and being in good physical health.

What this passage is clearly teaching us is that we must first attend to the prosperity of our soul in righteousness before focusing on prospering in financial matters. The reason is obvious; money is temporal but the soul is eternal. Unfortunately, most people, including many of God's people, fail to attend to the soul while they are pursuing wealth and riches. My humble and heartfelt prayer for all the Joseph's of Arimathea that God is raising all over the world is that they would prioritize the prosperity of their soul in the Lord at the same time they are amassing wealth. Jesus did not die for us to acquire more money; He died and shed His blood on the cross to redeem our lost souls from the power of sin and our banishment from the presence of God. I encourage every person reading this book to love God, His Kingdom and its righteousness more than you love what money can do for you.

LIVE TO GIVE!!!

It is more blessed to give than to receive. Acts 20:35

Finally, I want to encourage every person, and every Joseph of Arimathea who is reading this book to dedicate yourself to a life of giving. Wealth loses its true power and purpose when the person who has it refuses to embrace a life of giving to others, especially to those who find themselves in unfortunate circumstances. The Bible is littered with Scriptures that encourage God's people to give to the poor, widows and orphans. I'm so blessed to see many wealthy followers of Christ who are opening foundations that are designed to make a difference in peoples' lives. Giving purifies and protects the giver. Giving is the only cure to the cancer of greed and hording. Every Joseph of Arimathea must pray about supporting and financing a worthy cause that demonstrates God's love to a lost world of sin. Most importantly, every Joseph of Arimathea must not hesitate to use his or her wealth to fund the ministry of the Kingdom of God as well as the local church. The local church is still one of the most important tools God uses to reform society and disciple new converts to Christ.

PASS IT ON!

And I saw the dead, small and great, standing before God,[c] and books were opened. And another book was opened, which is the Book of Life. And the dead were judged according to their works, by the things which were written in the books. Revelation 20:12

Ever since I wrote my book The Order of Melchizedek a worldwide movement of people whom my book is transforming was unleashed. More life changing books that God had me write followed and thousands more people got impacted. However, The Joseph of Arimathea Calling is the first book that I have ever written that was directed to specifically helping the wealthy in the Body of Christ

194

understand the true purpose of their wealth. It's also a book written to aspiring and upcoming Kingdom businessmen and women, who sense a strong calling towards funding the Gospel of Jesus Christ. History has shown that books are very powerful instruments of change. I want to encourage every person reading this book to pray about buying an extra copy to give to someone else. Maybe you can pass on the one you are reading now to people you desire to influence for the Kingdom of God. Together we can change the world, one book at a time!!!

Endnotes

References have been made in this book from the writings of the following

1. http://www.bloomberg.com/billionaires/2016-09-30/cya

2. Munroe, Myles. Kingdom Principles. Shippensburg, PA: Destiny Image Publishers, 2006. p15

3. Britannia http://www.britannia.com/history/biographies/joseph.html

4. Myles, Francis. The Order of Melchizedek. Word and Spirit Books. Tulsa, OK

5. Television and Children. http://www.med.umich.edu/yourchild/topics/tv.htm

6. McCann Jami. No Time For Family? http://www.dailymail.co.uk/news/article-2363193/No-time-family-You-Parents-children-spend-hour-day-modern-demands.html

7. Bradshaw, Gordon. I See Thrones. Lakebay, WA: Kingdom House Publishing, 2015. Pgs 24 & 33.

8. Rushdoony, R.J. Law and Liberty. Vallecito, CA: Ross House Books, 2009. p 33

9. Bradshaw, Gordon. I See Thrones. Lakebay, WA: Kingdom House Publishing, 2015.

10. Ibid.

11. Holocaust Encyclopedia. "Oskar Schindler". https://www.ushmm.org/wlc/en/article.php?ModuleId=10005787

12. Greg Koukl. "To Bribe Or Not to Bribe" Stand to Reason., April 16, 2013. http://www.str.org/articles/to-bribe-or-not-to-bribe#.V_HNz_ArKhc

Sponsor a Book Program

The author has a deep desire to mail FREE copies of this book to pastors and business leaders in third world nations! Will you consider making a donation to help get these books into the hands of pastors and their leaders in underdeveloped countries?

To learn more about this program, please e-mail:

contactus@francismyles.com

INTERESTED IN SCHEDULING DR. FRANCIS MYLES?

The apostolic and prophetic ministry of Dr. Francis Myles is changing lives and transforming churches around the world. His life-changing messages on the Kingdom and the Order of Melchizedek are transforming the spiritual culture of churches and business corporations. As a successful businessman and spiritual mentor to heads of corporations, Dr. Francis Myles has a seasoned word which is helping activate many Kingdom business men and women into their God ordained ambassadorial assignments in the marketplace. If you are interested in having him at your church, business or conference, please e-mail us at the address below:

contactus@francismyles.com

ARE YOU INTERESTED IN USING THIS MATERIAL IN YOUR CHURCH'S BUSINESS LIFE GROUPS?

If you are interested in incorporating Dr. Francis Myles's book in your church's business life group program, please feel free to contact us at: contactus@francismyles.com

ARE YOU AN END-TIME JOSEPH?

- Do you feel called to something FAR GREATER than what you are currently doing in the marketplace?
- Have you achieved significant personal and business success, and still feel like that there is something missing?
- Do you desire to connect and network with other Kingdom-minded Joseph's across the world who are also awakening to their Kingdom destiny to father the "Movers and Shakers" of this world?

God is raising an end-time company of Josephs across the nations of the world. This is a prophetic company of men and women who are bringing the fathering spirit to the marketplace. It is a "new breed" without greed. It is a network of ordinary men and women who are bringing the power of an extraordinary God into corporate boardrooms and the corridors of government! It is a Kingdom network of Kingdom minded men and women who are using their

God given favor with their "Pharaoh" (business associates) to transform world systems into the Kingdoms of God and of His Christ.

If the above questions describe you and you would like additional information, we encourage you to contact us below:

e-mail: contactus@francismyles.com

WARNING: Our coalition of Kingdom businessmen and women will only cater to marketplace ministers who respect the role of the local church in their lives. We encourage members of our Kingdom Marketplace Coalition to be faithful members of a local church in the regions where God has planted them!

About the Author

Dr. Francis Myles is the Founder and Chairman of the Board of
The Order of Melchizedek Supernatural School of Ministry, Inc.

He is Founder and Chairman of the Board of Francis Myles International
www.francismyles.com

Dr. Francis Myles is also the Founding Apostle of Royal Priesthood
International Embassy based in Tempe, Arizona
www.rpfchurch.com

OTHER BOOKS BY THE AUTHOR

TITHES OF HONOR: Tithing under The Order of Melchizedek Breaking
Generational Curses Under the Order of Melchizedek
CHRIST JESUS: Our Royal High Priest
THE CONSCIOUSNESS OF NOW
The Spirit of Divine Interception
The Order of Melchizedek
Jumping The Line

For audio and MP3 versions of this book,
as well as other great titles by Dr. Francis Myles, please visit:
www.FrancisMyles.com.

61499315R00124

Made in the USA
Columbia, SC
24 June 2019